The

The Jacob Trossman Story

Marcy White

ISBN 978-0-9921436-0-2
Printed in the United States of America

BIO 026000: Biography + Autobiography: Personal Memoirs
FAM 012000: Family + Relationships: Children with Special Needs
FAM 034000: Family + Relationships: Parenting – General

Book design: Beeline Design & Communications

www.curepmd.com
www.theboywhocan.com

TABLE of CONTENTS

FOREWORD

Imagine running full tilt up a steep hill, breathless, wanting to stop, believing that a stretch of downhill relief lies ahead. Imagine your confusion, disappointment, fatigue, and mental and physical anguish when you reach the top of the hill only to realize that a few paces ahead lies yet another formidable ascent as the only path forward. Now imagine this relentless presentation of such barriers without certainty of what lies ahead, without your *a priori* consent as a willing participant, without the affirming cheers of supportive bystanders, but bearing on your shoulders the weight of a child's future and his limited opportunities for growth and development.

"The Boy Who Can" is an authentic and stark account of one such journey. This is the story of Marcy White, mother of three, and her eldest child, Jake, with complex needs as he navigates a relentless landscape of dunes, hills and mountains in his first decade of life, each time emerging wiser and stronger, but often bruised, battered and vulnerable. Herein lies the appeal of White's book: the narrative makes no attempt to align with the hero motif that too often epitomizes the lives of those with disability in popular media. White "tells it as it is" and claims no heroic victories. She openly acknowledges her own brokenness, weaknesses, fears, dashed hopes and disappointments. These are counterbalanced by glimpses of possibility and celebration in precious moments, such as Jake's first smile at eleven months and first taste of "cheesies." While this tension persists, the book manages to give the reader reprieve through White's ability to celebrate the joys that Jacob has brought into her life.

White depicts a pervasive tension between normalcy and her reality. She started the parental journey with an expected motherhood but instead found herself "stranded on an island," facing the foreign notion of mothering a non-verbal child with complex medical needs. With Jake's birth, she describes her life and how her hopes and dreams were transformed in an instant, never to be the same again. Indeed, White's reflections upon this discord between her expected and actual realities is poignant and painful. At one point, she recalls her avoidance of the sight of typically developing children in the neighborhood and her self-imposed social isolation as a mechanism of coping with the disparity between the life she "envisioned all those years ago" and her current reality.

Throughout the story, we see White's strength as a mother, advocate and caregiver. In Jacob's infancy, there is an elusive search for a diagnosis. Unfolding like a forensic mystery, White becomes the expert, digging into the family's medical genealogy when health care providers can offer no classification of Jake's condition. Her eventually successful search for a definitive diagnosis compounded with her horrific experiences with the system, such as those with the somnolent night nurse and verbally offensive community care worker, further intensify her resolve as the self-reliant, expert primary caregiver. Nonetheless, as the story develops, White, as a selfless mother, puts her son's psychosocial well-being before her own, and learns to embrace as she recounts, by necessity, her dependence on a village of people to care for Jacob.

Perhaps the most intimate internal conflict that is played out in the book is White's own need to be wanted, affirmed and validated by her son, not unlike the aspirations of many parents, juxtaposed with the feeling that outside her attendance to his basic needs, there is a dwindling number of special activities that her son wants to do with her. White wrestles with the heartbreaking observation that others have the luxury of interacting and playing with her son, while she is relegated to addressing his fundamental needs. She reluctantly acknowledges that Bracha, one of Jake's camp counsellors, can always calm her son, even when she cannot. While White concedes a pang of defeat and insufficiency at times, there is no doubt that she has transcended her own brokenness and vulnerability to recognize and marvel at how much her son has accomplished and to wonder in awe of those achievements yet to come.

Ultimately, it is White's tenacity in identifying such tensions within herself and her courage to embrace that which she cannot change while endeavoring to alter her own attitudes that exemplifies, I believe, what the late Dr. Viktor Frankl, Austrian psychiatrist and Holocaust survivor, described as the "defiant power of the human spirit."

Tom Chau, Senior Scientist and VP of Research,
Holland Bloorview Kids Rehabilitation Hospital

Jamie (left), Sierra (right) and Jacob

— JANUARY 2011 —

LETTER TO MY DAUGHTERS

Dear Sierra and Jamie;

You are too young for me to share this with you now but one day, when you are older, I will tell you how my heart hurt when you asked me why I loved your brother more than you. Your questions caught me off-guard and I'm not sure I expressed myself properly. I desperately need you to know that it is not true.

Being a parent is a constant juggling act, there are always so many balls in the air at risk of falling down and crashing to the floor. Parenting in a household with a "differently-abled" child like your brother is even more of a challenge, simply because his needs are different.

Jacob can't speak so he doesn't ask me to play with him. You do. Sometimes I feel guilty for spending more time with you, my mobile and verbal twins, than I do with your brother, who is dependent on others for absolutely everything.

I struggle with balancing my time between all my children. I am constantly asking myself how I can meet your needs without feeling that Jacob is constantly left out. At eight years old, you know so much about disease, more than any child your age should have to comprehend. You are aware that Pelizaeus-Merzbacher disease (PMD) is carried on the X chromosome and that you have two healthy Xs but Jake has a sick X that causes his PMD. You understand how PMD affects your brother, how he can't ask me a question, sit by himself or walk. You know that he can't eat like you do, and needs to be fed with the tube that was surgically implanted into his stomach when he was a few weeks old.

Everything is so hard for him, while you girls can ride your bikes, dance and eat the things you help me bake.

Although it may seem as if Jacob and I spend a lot of time together, relatively little of it is "fun" time, and in fact, we have little time alone during the week. We have our special allotment on Saturdays, but as you know, that it never starts off as a fun morning. As Emily's overnight nursing shift nears its end, I try to make sure your breakfast is prepared and a supply of bibs is packed in a bag for Jacob, all his things organized and easily accessible as soon as the front door closes behind her. I run through my mental list of things that need to be done before the craziness begins in earnest. From the moment Emily walks out of our house until your big brother is fastened in his car seat, you listen to Jacob crying and screaming. Our neighbors must wonder what awful torture I am inflicting on him. And I see you sitting there with your hands over your ears, trying to block out the noise. When you realize that won't work, you begin to dance around in front of your brother in an eager attempt to console him and elicit a smile. You probably don't realize this, but I stop what I'm doing and watch you. My heart swells with pride when I see you trying to help Jacob but I also feel like crying—I wish you didn't have to watch your brother struggle so hard to make himself understood. You should be able to enjoy a lazy weekend morning at home in your pajamas, cuddling in bed with your parents, not watching us run up and down the stairs, organizing your older sibling's medical paraphernalia. Unfortunately—for all of us, but especially for Jacob—this is not what our life is like.

In order for me to hang out with Jacob, we have to leave our house. He screams incessantly when I try to play with him at home while you are present. As soon as we leave, he calms down. I have his full attention and together we can enjoy the outing. Maybe Jake knows that I can't tune everyone else out at home and that he is forced to share my focus with you, the cats, and all the other millions of things that distract me. Regardless of the reason, when we are out, alone, we have fun. It's "Mommy and Jakey" time.

And we have our weekly swimming. You know how your big brother loves the pool and has learned to swim somewhat independently, surprising the lifeguards and making us all so proud of him. If I'm nearby and not in the water with him, Jake complains and is unable to enjoy the activity; however, if I am in the water, reminding him to move his arms and kick his legs and encouraging his effort, he beams. He giggles and I feel his arms tighten around my neck in a delicious and intentional hug. After our 45-minute swim, as we are getting dressed and ready to leave, my back aches. Holding him, walking with him on the ramp into and out of the pool, is taxing on a body that has endured more lifting and twisting than it can handle. But watching Jake swim the length of the pool, seeing his little legs break the surface during a kick and listening to his squeal of delight when his hand touches the wall at the end of a lap, is worth every pain.

After those outings, I return feeling like I have spent some quality time with my first born, the child I often believe does not get enough of my undivided attention.

It is so much easier for me to play with you, my beautiful darlings. You express your thoughts and questions so eloquently, and you don't need me to help you move your leg if it slides off the footrest of your chair. I am in awe of your intelligence and imagination. I love watching you play elaborate games with your dolls as you create different experiences for them. I can sit and listen to your stories for hours. I marvel at the various masterpieces you create for me, each one an incredible work of art.

I drive you to and from your school while Jacob is bussed to and from his. I bathe you and help put on your pajamas. I tuck you into bed at night and comfort you when you wake with a nightmare. A caregiver bathes your brother because he is too heavy for me to carry. I am terrified that I might drop his wet and slippery body during the short transfer from his special shower chair to his changing table. The same caregiver puts Jacob to sleep while I'm with you, listening to stories about your day. I crawl into bed with Jake for a few minutes of cuddling before he falls asleep. And it's the nurse in his room who administers his medication and helps ease him back to sleep in the middle of the night when he wakes up with a fever.

But, when I put you into bed this evening, your question sliced through me like a jagged edge of broken glass: Why do you love Jacob more than us?

The answer, quite simply, is that I don't love him more than you. And I don't love you more than him. I love all of you the same. I just have to show it differently.

all my love,
Mommy

"Life does not have to be perfect
to be wonderful."

Annette Funicello

INTRODUCTION

It took eight long years but I never gave up.

Like most parents, I had eagerly anticipated my child's first words. Unlike most parents, I was told by doctors—over and over again—that my son would never talk. I didn't accept it. I couldn't. Despite Jacob's many health and developmental challenges, I knew he had a lot to say. For years, I searched for ways to help my son express himself. I was determined to find the key that would unlock a world of communication for him.

By the time Jacob was four years old, he knew how to consistently respond "yes" or "no" when given a choice. At the time, I thought that was great. He was making his wishes known; he could have a say in what toys he wanted to play with or where he wanted to go. But when Jacob's younger twin sisters were learning to express themselves, I noticed how their statements would jump around. One minute they'd be talking about a doll and the next they'd be telling me about something they'd watched on television earlier in the day.

That got me thinking: if Jacob's mind worked the same way, it was no wonder he sometimes got so frustrated. When he was trying to say something, I'd ask a few yes or no questions. After the second or third no, he would lose it and then scream and scream in frustration. The yes and no questions were too limiting because Jacob could only tell me what he wanted *if* I asked the right question. He needed more.

I had so many dreams about Jacob's first words. I would wake during the night filled with the fresh memory of a conversation with my son, only to realize it was an illusion. As I lay in my bed, the pleasant feeling would quickly be replaced by a heavy sense of sadness. I was awake, not dreaming, and Jacob was still unable to speak—filled with the usual frustrations.

It was August of 2010 when I wheeled my son into a small room near the elevator bank in the children's rehabilitation center. I noticed that there were no windows. The walls were painted a typical institutional beige and devoid of pictures. The only furniture was a table and a few hard chairs. I positioned Jacob in his wheel-chair at the long end of the rectangular table and sat down next to him. Tom Chau, a biomedical engineer, sat across from us, fac-ing Jacob. The others hovered by the doorway. They were all eager to see what would happen, but they kept a respectful distance, not wanting to overwhelm or scare my son.

I knew from experience that Jacob hated listening to people talk about him. I was nervous and worried about how he would react during this consultation. There were so many people in the room and I was really hoping they wouldn't walk away thinking that they had wasted their time. I was prepared for Jacob's usual unrestrained screaming and gathered apologies in my mind so I would be ready. I prayed Jacob would be able to hold it together and co-operate for at least a few minutes, but years of appointments had taught me not to expect too much.

I certainly wasn't expecting this meeting to be a pinnacle moment in our lives.

After a brief introduction to the team of software engineers assembled by the doorway, Tom gave Jacob an iPod that had been specifically designed for him. It looked like a regular iPod Touch, but it featured a jack that attached to a Jellybean switch—a palm-sized device that resembled a green M&M. It wasn't the only difference. Instead of music, this iPod was programmed with messages from the communication book that Jacob's family, teachers and therapists routinely used with him.

Using the communication book is laborious and slow because it requires the person who is with Jacob to recognize his cues and make sure the book is nearby. If it seems like Jacob wants something, we say: "Jacob, do you have something to say?" When he nods his head yes, we scroll through a series of questions, in a specific order, until the desired statement is reached. If he is uncomfortable, for example, Jacob will respond affirmatively when asked that question. Only then is someone able to realize that he is in pain or wants to be taken out of his wheelchair.

Tom explained to Jacob that if he pressed the Jellybean switch, the iPod would scroll through his familiar messages. When Jacob heard the message he wanted, he was to push his switch again and the iPod would announce his choice. Jake was told that he didn't need to wait for someone to ask him questions; if he had something to say, he could simply select the choice himself.

Much to my surprise, Jacob listened intently to the entire explanation. When Tom placed the switch on the table in front of him, Jacob slowly raised his hand and listened to the messages. After a few tries, he figured out how the machine worked.

The room was silent. I leaned over and asked Jacob if he had something to say. He pushed the switch once to start the machine and then again when the right category of phrases was announced. Finally, with all the effort he could muster—any type of movement is painfully slow and hard for him—he lowered his chubby little hand onto the green switch. The mechanical voice of the iPod, a proxy for my son, stated: "I want a great big hug."

It took me a moment to process what had just occurred. As my eyes filled with tears, I reached over the side of Jacob's wheelchair and gave him the biggest hug I could. While I was holding him, I heard the voices of all the naysayers in my head, telling me that this moment would never arrive. I wanted to shout at them. I wanted to point out how wrong they had been and admonish them for try- ing to dash my hope that one day Jacob would be able to share his thoughts. I wanted to call everyone I knew and tell them what had just happened. My son was finally able to communicate and the first thing he chose to say was that he wanted a hug from me. My insides felt like they were going to explode with love and pride.

When I pulled away to look at Jacob's face and tell him how proud I was of him, I wasn't sure if his enormous grin was because he'd received the hug he requested or because he knew that I finally understood what he wanted.

It hardly mattered. On that warm summer day, in that small beige room filled with strangers, my eight-year-old son uttered his first words.

• • •

I had no idea how my safe and insular world would be tossed, shaken and dropped unceremoniously on its head with the first breath of my first child in May 2002.

It was Jacob's birth and early struggle for life that led me to my unequivocal vocation, the one I never thought I would have. It wasn't a dramatic shift, despite what you might expect. Instead, the realization gnawed at my brain like a persistent cat that wants a head rub. As I watched Jacob fight for his life and baffle the medical professionals who were at a loss to explain his illness, I knew I had to stand up and advocate for my little boy. I consciously closed all the doors that I had previously propped open in my life. My hard-earned university degrees and flourishing career were ushered out as all of my energy and determination was directed toward my family. As Jacob's symptoms snowballed, I emphatically decided I wasn't going back to work in the investment industry. How could I, when my son's health was so precarious and his every breath was a noisy struggle for air? It wasn't something I ever wavered on—Jacob's well-being was my categorical focus. Helping him grow and recover was my single-minded vision, and nothing was going to sway me from this path.

Ironically, the profession I'd once consciously steered away from—the one I decided against because of my discomfort around sickness—was the one in which I ended up immersing myself. I dusted off my anatomy textbooks and spent a lot of time reading medical books online. I earned a Ph.D. in Jacob.

I was relentless when I was told that we would likely never receive a diagnosis. I scoured the Internet, read countless medical articles and contacted handfuls of experts across the globe. Eventually, my husband Andrew and I figured out what was causing our son's unusual symptoms.

As Jacob was closing in on his first year, we received a shattering diagnosis. Jacob had Pelizaeus-Merzbacher disease (PMD), an incurable and rare neurodegenerative disease. Jacob's prognosis was grim. The doctors told me that he would never speak or sit independently. His symptoms would worsen as he aged.

Once the shock wore off, I determined to do whatever was humanly possible to find a cure for this horrible disease. I was not ready to sit on the sidelines and watch as PMD slowly ravaged my son's body. He deserved more. And as his mother, I was not going to let anything or anyone stop me from giving him the best chance at a full and happy life.

Slowly and subtly, Jacob became my teacher, steering me in directions I could not have imagined. I learned how to be a more tolerant and accepting person. I found the strength to stand up for my son and the courage to combat ignorance. Through him, I was led to a community filled with good, kind and loving people who accepted my son without hesitation.

Never in a million years would I have imagined my life taking the path it has. Never in a million years would I have wanted it to. Given a "do over," I would wish for nothing more than a fully healthy Jacob, with no problem more serious than a bruised knee or hurt feelings. But wishes don't always come true, and sometimes we have to adjust.

This book is about adjustment. It's about taking what life throws at you and doing your best to cope (and sometimes even thrive). It's about figuring out what's important, even if that turns out to be one hundred per cent different from what you'd imagined. And most importantly, it's about being willing to learn—even if your teacher is thirty-three years younger than you and, at age eight, just learning to talk.

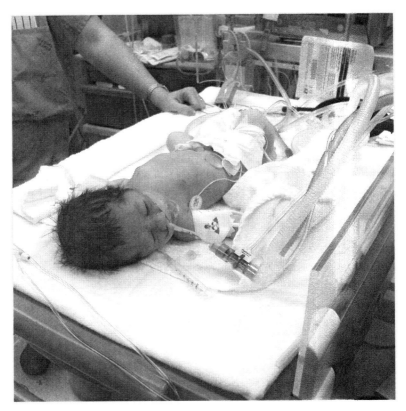

Jacob, a couple of hours after his birth, in the Resuscitation Room

— MAY 15, 2002 —

*"Learning is not compulsory
but neither is survival."*

W. Edwards Deming

CHAPTER 1

OFF TO A ROUGH START

My world was shattered with Jacob's first breath.

I was a few days past my due date and the doctor had suggested inducing me before the first long weekend of the summer. He was going away for the holiday and made the suggestion so that he could be the one to deliver my baby.

As much as I liked the idea of going into labour when the baby decided it was time, there were reasons to consider being induced. Both my husband and I liked our doctor and very much wanted him to be there for the birth. And my parents had come to Toronto a few days earlier and were going to stay until their first grandchild was born. I was torn but eventually agreed.

I barely slept the night before, I was so nervous. I had a large suitcase filled with diapers, wipes, gender-neutral white, yellow and green onesies, and the yellow blanket I'd been wrapped in when I came home from the hospital more than three decades earlier. I knew that I'd over-packed, but I didn't care. I was too excited!

I placed the list of people I wanted to call after the birth and multiple copies of our well-thought-out birth plan in the front zipper pocket of my bag. I even packed a novel, crazily thinking I'd have time to read.

As we walked to our car in the early hours of May 15, 2002, the sun was starting to rise. My husband, Andrew, wheeled my overstuffed suitcase down the driveway as I clutched my pillow. I'd been warned about the hospital's uncomfortable pillows and was coming prepared with my own.

It was a pleasant spring morning, a perfect day to have a baby, I thought. I remarked to Andrew how civilized the induction process seemed. I wasn't in any pain and my water hadn't broken. My labour hadn't even begun, yet we were on our way to the hospital, the freshly installed infant car seat securely fastened in the back of our vehicle, ready to bring our new addition home the next day.

We arrived at the Labour and Delivery floor of Mount Sinai Hospital at seven a.m. We were told to wait until a room was readied for us. As I sat down, I looked at the pink sweater I'd worn so many times over the past few months. The next time I put it on, I thought with a smile, the buttons wouldn't be straining so hard to stay closed.

Fifteen minutes later, we were escorted down the hall into a huge room. It wasn't one of the renovated delivery suites we'd visited during our hospital tour a few weeks earlier, but it was enormous and would easily accommodate our families, who were planning on spending the day with us.

After handing a copy of my birth plan to the nurse, I reviewed it with her. The salient points were pretty straightforward: I wanted an epidural when the pain rose to an intolerable level; I wanted to hold my baby immediately following the birth; and I wanted to breastfeed. If someone had told me then that the only item on my plan that would actually happen was the administration of the pain medication, I wouldn't have believed it.

I changed into the standard-issue blue hospital gown and was hooked up to machines so the nurses could monitor my baby's heart rate. An IV was started in my right arm and I was given the medication needed to induce delivery. I was told that I was already 3 cm dilated, which meant that I would likely have a baby by the end of the day. Andrew and I looked at each other and smiled. After nine months of anxious waiting, it was almost impossible to believe that our baby would be with us in a matter of hours.

I'd had a wonderfully uneventful pregnancy and loved watching my belly undulate every time the baby moved. I loved the feeling of life growing inside me and the sense that my body knew exactly what to do to take care of this new being. As happy as I'd been during the pregnancy, though, it was time to proceed to the next stage—it was time to meet my child. I couldn't wait to become a mother, but underneath all that excitement, I was terrified of going through the birthing process.

Throughout the day, Andrew sent our friends frequent email updates from the hospital, describing how my labour was progressing: "4 cm now, getting an epidural"; "7 cm now, getting close"; "fully dilated, ready to push." Then the emails stopped.

When it was time to start pushing, the people who had congregated in our room were asked to leave. My parents, grandmother, brother and in-laws walked to the waiting room to anxiously await the birth of the newest family member.

The nurses readied the bed and the doctor arrived. To my surprise and relief, I wasn't feeling any pain. In fact, I was thoroughly enjoying the whole process. The nurses placed extra blankets on my stomach when the baby's head was crowning, preparing for the moment when my child would be wrapped and cleaned right on me. An air of anticipation filled the room; it was thrilling.

And then the world as I knew it came crashing to an end. In an instant, everything changed.

• • •

"I've never seen anything like this before" were the first words I heard from the doctor after my son was born. I listened to the donkey-like sound coming from the end of the bed and tried to make sense of what was happening. This was nothing like the traditional newborn cries I heard on the episodes of *A Baby Story* that I'd watched so frequently throughout my pregnancy.

No doubt sensing my confusion and concern, Andrew left my side to see his son. Playing the role of the new father to the hilt, he took photos of our baby on the table while the doctors worked. It was what he'd planned to do—photograph his son immediately after his birth—and we hadn't been given a reason to deviate from the plan. In the scenario we'd imagined so many times, our baby was a healthy pink colour with limbs flailing, not pasty blue-grey with a grossly heaving chest.

From where I was lying on the delivery table, it looked like our son's ribs were constructed of rubber. With every breath he took, his ribcage would collapse, appearing to fold in half with each noisy inhalation. Later, I would hear the doctors and nurses call this unusual, noisy breathing a stridor. It was a term I'd never heard before, and one that I still wish I didn't know.

I was in a daze. Things were spinning out of control and there was no way I could stop it. I had just given birth—that much had gone according to plan—but my baby was not wrapped in the warm flannel blankets that were still waiting for him on my belly. He was on the other side of the room and one of the hospital staff was on the phone asking for assistance.

As I watched, not knowing what to do or say, my son was bundled up and handed to a respiratory therapist, who was preparing to run out the door with him. My doctor, who was still finishing with the delivery, asked that my child be brought to me, "so the mother can see her baby." I was given less than five seconds to see my son—too quick for me to focus on the details of his tiny face. A moment later, he was gone, taken to receive the emergency treatment he would need to survive.

More than anything, I wanted to jump up and follow. But there was no way I could; the epidural had taken care of that. The fact that I didn't panic in those first few minutes is a miracle—one that I attribute to the calm and professional manner of my seasoned doctor. Looking back, I don't think I fully comprehended the gravity of the situation. I was probably in shock. Not only had I just given birth but something had gone horribly wrong. I didn't know what, but I certainly knew that we were dealing with an unexpected crisis.

While I was waiting for the effects of the epidural to wear off, Andrew left me in the care of two nurses so he could check on our baby. As they cleaned up the room, the two women did their best to reassure me. One mentioned that breathing issues are not uncommon and that my baby was receiving excellent care. I don't remember asking any questions or demanding answers. I was scared silent.

As Andrew raced down the hall behind the respiratory therapists, he passed our family in the waiting room. Expecting to hear whether we'd had a boy or a girl, they were blindsided when Andrew blurted out "there's something wrong with him" and continued down the hall. That was how our family learned that our new addition was a boy.

When Andrew returned to my bedside a brief time later our families were in the room, seated in a semi-circle around the foot of my bed. Andrew explained that the doctors were baffled. They didn't know what was going on and were still trying to figure it out.

I am normally a very inquisitive person, and come to situations armed with an undergraduate degree in Anatomical Science. But I couldn't think of a single question to ask, other than the obvious "what's wrong with him?" and "will he be okay?" Nobody had any answers.

As our families chatted quietly, my mind drifted back to the birthing plan. Our son's arrival was supposed to be routine. I hadn't expected any deviations from my detailed birth plan, let alone a life-threatening complication. I tried to take in everything that had happened, but it was no use. I couldn't believe that my baby was in another part of the hospital, fighting to stay alive. I didn't want to accept that it was real, but the painful sound of his breathing reverberated in my ears.

I pushed away the tray of food that was brought to me. How could the nurse expect me to eat when the thought of food made me nauseous? How was I supposed to have an appetite when I hadn't even really seen my baby yet? All I wanted was to hold him and know that he was alright.

Finally, after what seemed like forever but was probably only a little while, I was wheeled into the Resuscitation Room. I held onto the bag of fluid that was still being infused into my body through the IV in my arm and stood up on shaky legs to meet my son. He was so small, dwarfed by the machines surrounding him and nearly lost in the tangle of tubes and wires coming out of him. He was lying on a white towel draped over a small examination table. There was one tube in his throat and another one in his nose, and both were taped in place with large strips of adhesive. A machine was breathing for him. My baby's body was peppered with electrodes to monitor his heart rate. A tiny white vinyl blood pressure cuff with royal blue writing was wrapped around his right bicep and an IV line was secured to the back of his left hand. A rectangular piece of foam was taped from his wrist to his palm to prevent him from dislodging the IV with any movements he might make.

I couldn't hold him—nobody could, the respiratory therapist told me. He had too many things connected to him. He barely moved. I couldn't believe that he was mine, and that this was how we were meeting.

I stared at him, not even noticing who else was in the room with us. I tried to drink in the scene with my eyes and process what was happening. Looking back on it now, it's as if the first night of Jacob's life was unfolding in slow motion, as if I was in a nightmare from which I would soon rouse.

That night my baby was transferred to the Neonatal Intensive Care Unit (NICU) and I was given a room on the post-delivery floor, not far from where my son was fighting for his life. Once the nurses were briefed on what little information was known, I was allowed to see him again.

My newborn son, only a few hours old, was in an enclosed incubator near the entrance to the unit. At six pounds, eight ounces, he was the biggest baby in a room filled mostly with premies. I slid my hands into the round openings at the side of the box so I could touch him. My heart hurt and my mind was reeling. I gently stroked his full head of dark hair and counted his tiny fingers and toes. I studied his face and wondered if he looked like me.

He was sleeping on his stomach and my first thought was that he looked peaceful, but helpless. He was still connected to so many machines! Then, something inside me clicked. I turned to the nurse in a near panic and asked why he was on his stomach.

Everything I'd read about caring for newborns stated that placing a baby on his stomach was wrong; in fact, it was the most danger-ous position possible. The parenting books, which offered differ-ing opinions on so many things, were unanimous about this. The nurse gently touched my shoulder and explained that it was easier for my baby to breathe in that position. She said that he was hooked up to monitors to keep track of his vital signs and that his sleeping position would not subject him to any additional danger. When she told me that the ventilator was breathing for him, it dawned on me how ridiculous my fear was. He had much bigger problems than his sleeping position.

Still, seeing him resting quietly helped me feel a bit calmer since he didn't seem to be in distress. I allowed myself a fleeting thought: maybe he was out of danger.

Later that night, Mindy Black, the on-call resident from The Hospital for Sick Children (HSC) and a high school friend whom I had not seen in years, arrived to examine my son. He was resting but still intubated, the machine down his throat breathing for him. It was decided that the following day he would be taken to HSC and the head of otolaryngology (an ear, nose and throat specialist) would examine him.

At the end of her investigation, Mindy asked if we had any fam-ily history of breathing issues. Andrew and I knew that my grand-mother had had children who died in infancy but we were uncer-tain of the details. Mindy came back to my hospital room where our families had assembled and Andrew asked my grandmother for any details she could provide.

My grandmother said that her first son had a malformed larynx and died shortly after birth. We didn't realize it at the time, but that one piece of information would be critical in helping us uncover what was wrong with Jacob. It started us through a maze that would take more than nine years and a lawsuit to unfold.

When the conversation was over and Mindy left to attend to someone else, our families stayed in the room. I don't recall the specifics of the conversation, but there were a lot of statements such as: "I'm sure it will all be okay" and "he'll be fine."

Nobody wanted to believe anything else.

It was during this time that Andrew and I announced our son's name. It was a name we had decided on shortly after learning I was pregnant. Jacob. He was named after my maternal grandfather, Jack, who had passed away three years earlier. Jack was one of the most thoughtful and gentle people we knew. There wasn't a soul alive who had anything but wonderful things to say about him and we thought that giving our child his name would be a fitting tribute to the man we'd adored.

As happy as we were with our choice and as pleased as we were to finally be sharing it with our families, the revealing of Jacob's name was a bittersweet moment. Everyone knew how much my grandfather meant to us and how thrilled he would have been to meet his namesake, but the uncertainty of Jacob's survival cast a somber shadow.

· · ·

The following day, Jacob and I were wheeled into the basement of Mount Sinai through a maze of tunnels that connect the downtown Toronto hospitals to each other. Throughout the fifteen-minute journey to HSC, we quietly followed two nurses who pushed Jacob in an incubator on wheels. I felt weak. I wasn't allowed to walk through the long tunnel, no surprise considering I had given birth less than twelve hours earlier and my body was still healing. But the wheelchair just underlined the fact that I had no control over what was happening. I was simply going where the doctors told me to go. I wasn't accustomed to being so passive but my mind was still reeling with the enormity of the situation. I was paralyzed with fear. I couldn't think straight. I couldn't muster the strength to demand more information or ask intelligent questions.

I felt as if I were living a scene in a scary movie—the dark and damp of the secret passageway seemed so fitting for the horror that my life had become. Our families were with us, but I don't remember much conversation taking place. Everyone was lost in his or her own thoughts and fears.

Jacob, still asleep, was settled in to the NICU at HSC and we waited about twenty minutes for the doctor to arrive. When he showed up at Jacob's bedside, flanked by half a dozen students and residents, he swiftly removed the tube that was in Jacob's throat helping him breathe. When my son started making the donkey-like stridor, the doctor administered a steroid, placed him back in his bed on his tummy and watched as he fell asleep. Jacob was breathing quietly, on his own.

The doctor, who spoke with the confidence of a seasoned professional, told us that the worst was over and that we would probably never know what had caused Jacob's breathing trouble. He assured us that our son was fine and recommended that he go home the following day with us.

Our small group let out a collective sigh of relief, but I was guarded. I wasn't convinced that my son was out of danger. He'd had a stridor when he woke up moments earlier and had required medication to quiet him. But I desperately wanted to believe Jacob was going to be okay. I wanted to go home and begin our life together.

We headed back through the tunnels to Mount Sinai. In my head, I reasoned that the doctor had to know what he was talking about. He was the head of otolaryngology, after all. Never mind that the nurses in the NICU reported that each time Jacob woke up during the night and cried he had a stridor. I put it out of my mind. The doctor was right. The doctor is always right.

I hung onto that thought until later in the afternoon when Jacob woke up crying and struggling to breathe. Each breath sounded like a donkey braying and his chest wall kept folding inwards, as though his rib cage was touching his spine every time he inhaled. It was painful to watch and it made one thing perfectly clear: Jacob was not out of danger. His breathing was still laboured. It was not normal. Something was not right.

Nevertheless, the nurses started preparing the discharge documents. As far as they were concerned, the doctor from HSC had said Jacob was fine and therefore, he was going home—never mind that they knew something was wrong. I was astounded. Despite the evidence of a problem with Jacob's breathing, they chose to stay quiet. No one wanted to challenge the authority of the physician who had clearly misjudged the severity of Jacob's stridor.

Jacob was one day old when I stood up to the nurses in the quiet of the NICU for the first time. I pleaded with them to reconsider sending Jacob home; it was obvious he wasn't stable. When my requests were refused, I knew what I had to do. For the first time since Jacob's birth, I took control. I was not about to stand by and do nothing when something was clearly wrong with my son.

I demanded to see the on-call physician at Mount Sinai. I told the nurses that I wasn't taking my son home until he was stable. My limbs were trembling while I waited for the physician to arrive but I held firm. I brought the doctor over to my son's incubator. I had him listen to Jacob's breathing and watch his collapsing chest. The doctor acknowledged that Jacob was too ill to be discharged and agreed to contact HSC and arrange for another doctor to examine my little boy.

It was Friday, the start of the first long weekend of the summer and the hospitals were operating with fewer staff. We were told that Jacob would stay in the NICU at Mount Sinai until he could be seen by a specialist at HSC on Tuesday. Frustrated with the four-day delay, I realized that I had no choice. I took some small comfort from the fact that I was not being discharged until then, so I could stay by my son's bedside. That, at least, was a tiny piece of good news.

Slowly but surely I was coming out of the shock that had followed Jacob's birth. I was starting to process what was happening and, as scary as it was, I knew what I had to do. I needed to stand up for my baby. I had to do what I believed was right for him. After all, I was his mother.

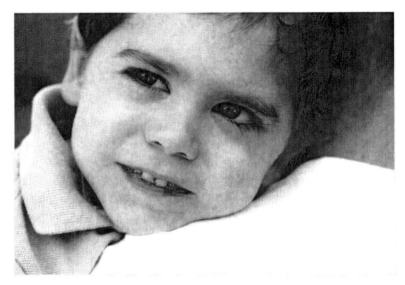

Jacob at 2 years old

— SUMMER 2004 —

"Anyone can give up,
it's the easiest thing in the world to do.
But to hold it together
when everyone else would understand
if you fell apart,
that's true strength."

Christopher Reeves

CHAPTER 2

SOMETHING ISN'T RIGHT

When I entered the NICU to feed Jacob on his second morning, I was surprised to see yet another tube running out of his tiny body. This one was a two-foot-long naso-gastric (NG) tube. It emerged from his nose and was taped to his soft cheek with a white gauze-like bandage that covered almost the entire right side of his face. The nurse, noticing my appalled reaction, explained that this tube would function to deliver my pumped breast milk directly into his stomach because he couldn't swallow without choking. I watched silently as the milk slid into his body, drip by drip.

Looking back, I'm not sure what I would have said or done had someone discussed the placement of the NG tube with me when the doctors considered this intervention. At the time, I didn't really understand what was going on since my mind wasn't willing to process the details of what my eyes were seeing. I now understand that without the feeding tube in his nose, Jacob might have choked to death on my milk, or would have continued to lose weight and the strength to fight for his life. Nobody explained that he might never be able to swallow or that he would require a tube to feed him for the rest of his life. Even at the time I thought it was strange that such a serious action was taken without Andrew's or my consent. I didn't say anything because I didn't want to alienate the people who were working so hard to care for my little fighter. I had only been a parent for a day while the doctors and nurses had so much more experience. I deferred to them without consciously being aware of it and didn't question their decision. This time.

The NICU had a strict two-person maximum visiting policy. I rarely left Jacob's side. Andrew and the rest of our families, who spent almost as much time at the hospital as we did, took turns being the second visitor. It was during these long days and nights that I learned how to feed my son. I had never heard of tube feeding, and at first it was scary and unnatural. I oscillated between thinking I didn't want to do it and knowing that I had to.

The process was so involved! First, I made myself comfortable in a high-backed chair. Then a nurse placed my frail son in my arms and untangled the mass of wires that invariably got mixed up during the transfer from his bed to me. Once Jacob was safely in my embrace, the nurse taped a vial of milk securely to the back of my chair and attached the small opening to the tubing that led to his NG tube. I looked at my son, learning the details of his face, and my eyes moved to the milk that dripped slowly into his stomach. I kept thinking that this wasn't the way he should be eating. Why couldn't he just swallow? My stomach churned as I forced my eyes to follow the length of the tube from the vial of milk until it disappeared into the hollow of his nostril. I wanted to run away.

I also recall thinking that I couldn't handle this. When I was in university, students who majored in Anatomical Science typically envisioned themselves entering the medical profession. I had no such aspirations although I enjoyed the courses and my grades were strong. I never considered being a doctor because I hated hospitals and was terrified of being around sick people. Sitting in the NICU with my baby brought back those feelings and made me remember why I consciously elected to forgo a medical career. I was squeamish and didn't think I could overcome my fear to learn how to comfort and care for my painfully frail child. And just when

I started to become upset, Jacob began to choke. A nurse took him from my arms and did something to help him breathe. I couldn't bring myself to watch and I sat there helplessly, trembling in the seat. The nurse never left my side during his feeding, and for that I was grateful because I was too scared to be alone with him. This was not how I envisioned nourishing my newborn. The images I had of quietly breastfeeding my child while I was seated in the pale green rocking chair in his room painfully flashed through my mind as I sat with Jacob amidst the beeps and hums of the NICU.

Two days after Jacob's birth, my doctor could no longer find a reason to keep me in the hospital and I was to be discharged. But I didn't want to leave without my baby so the nurses arranged for me to move down the hall. This new room was closer to the NICU, a space reserved for parents of the sickest children, those who couldn't be assured that their babies would still be alive in the morning. I forced those thoughts out of my head and focused on my relief at knowing that I could stay by Jake's side.

The subsequent days blended together since the routine was always the same. I would spend as much time as possible next to Jacob's crib, leaving every three hours to express breast milk so that he would have it to "drink." During the twenty minutes that I was tethered to the pump, one of our relatives would take my seat by my son's bed. Jacob was never without a family member's company.

When the long weekend was finally behind us, it was time for Jacob's appointment with an Ear, Nose and Throat specialist at HSC, a doctor who specialized in pediatric airways. Once again, Jacob was readied for the trek through the tunnels. This time I was able to walk beside his incubator to this appointment. Our parents met us at Dr. Forte's office.

It was a very brief exam. Andrew stayed with Jacob while the doctor stuck another tube down my baby's throat, this time for the purpose of looking around his airway. As much as I wanted to hold my son during this invasive test, I couldn't. I was terrified and didn't want to watch, grateful that my husband had none of my squeamishness and was able to witness every test that Jacob had to endure.

At the conclusion of the appointment, Dr. Forte, a large, burly man with huge hands and a surprisingly gentle touch, explained that Jacob's vocal cords were paralyzed. This condition was so rare that the specialists at HSC had not seen it in more than fifteen years. The paralysis explained his stridor, the way his chest collapses when he inhales and his eating challenges. We learned that Jake's vocal cords were paralyzed in the median, or middle, position. This allowed him to make sounds but impeded his airway, making breathing difficult and swallowing too dangerous—the cords did not close to protect his airway when he swallowed. He was at constant risk of aspiration, where milk, or even his own saliva, could "go down the wrong pipe" and end up in his lungs, which could be fatal.

Dr. Forte told us that he would admit Jacob to the NICU at HSC immediately so that further tests could be conducted to determine the underlying cause of this new and unusual finding.

I didn't know it then, but the doctor took my parents and mother-in-law aside and explained to them that Jacob was dangerously ill. He told them that Andrew and I would need a tremendous amount of support from our families. What he didn't realize was that our families were already there with us, with each laboured breath my son—their grandson, nephew and cousin—took.

As the paperwork to admit Jacob to the NICU at HSC was being processed, our parents stayed with Jacob while Andrew and I returned to my room at Mount Sinai to collect my things. When we returned about an hour later, Jacob was moved into a room with three other infants, and I was told that a Family Room was reserved for Andrew and me at the end of the hall so we could stay overnight.

The following day, however, we were informed that all the Family Rooms were booked and we would not have a place to sleep. Our only options were to go home, without our baby, or spend the long hours sitting in a chair by Jacob's crib. As much as I hated leaving him, I knew that without sleep, I would be of no use to him the following day. The NICU's nurse-to-patient ratio of 1:2 made the logical part of the decision more palatable but it was still heartbreaking.

That evening, in the car for the first time since driving to the hospital to give birth to my son, I couldn't help but notice the vacant blue and white checkered car seat, carefully installed a few weeks ago by Andrew. It felt so wrong to be leaving the hospital without my baby safely buckled into the Transport Canada approved rear-facing bucket seat. Though I didn't think it possible, I felt even worse when I walked into my house and saw the empty room with the brand new crib, changing table and rocking chair.

Over the next few days, Jacob was seen by a variety of doctors, residents and students. Without asking for permission or explaining the reasons, people in white coats would come up to my son's bedside to touch and poke him, or shine lights in his face. I was a new mother, inexperienced and uncertain about my son's survival. I wanted the specialists to examine him; I wanted them to figure out what was wrong and then fix him. I wanted my son to be well and did not want to stand in their way. I knew Jacob's health was precarious, but I didn't consider the possibility that his issues wouldn't be "fixed". I firmly believed that once the doctors arrived at their diagnosis, we would begin the process of curing him. It was comforting to know that we were at a world-renowned children's hospital staffed with leading pediatric experts and where, according to the Sick Kids Telethon we watched on television, "miracles happen every day."

I was often asked to leave the room while the medical group discussed my son at his crib side. It didn't take long for me to resent this practice because I felt I needed to know what they were talking about. A few times I overheard their discussions and noticed errors in the information exchange. Never one to bite my tongue, I piped up and tried to explain what really happened but I was often rebuked. For instance, they did not want to hear that Jacob was suctioned three times, once when the nurse assigned to him was on her break and therefore was not aware that her replacement had already done it. I watched in anger and surprise as the group took a few steps farther away so I wouldn't hear the balance of their conversation. I was frustrated every time I was excluded from conversations and kept thinking of it as a grown-up version of broken telephone, with the wrong information inevitably being communicated. I was the constant, the one who was by Jacob's side while a revolving stream of nurses and doctors assigned to his care came and went. Despite my lack of medical knowledge, my understanding of my baby was growing exponentially. I was gaining an important type of expertise, one that was just as necessary to his survival. Yet I felt shut out.

It was so hard to get details. I would pick up Jacob's chart and peruse the scribbles, one of the ways I tried to keep up with what was going on. To the dismay of the nurses and doctors, I pointed out errors, such as when he was last fed or how frequently he vomited. But once a tidbit made it into "the file," it was virtually impossible to change.

When Jacob was one week old, I held him while I was sitting in a rocking chair next to his crib. I looked around at the place that was starting to become familiar and saw Jacob's bed, with a red string tied to one of the bars. According to the Kabbalah, the study of Jewish mysticism, the colour red represents protective powers against negative energy and evil. I wished that the little piece of string could really ward off anything bad from happening to my baby. There was a little red bear stationed at the foot of his mattress, another superstitious bit of red to keep my tiny son safe. With tears streaming down my face, I quietly sang happy birthday to my seven-day-old son.

· · ·

Around this time, Andrew returned to work at the software development start-up firm he was spearheading. Before the birth, our plan was for him to spend the baby's first week at home with us. Instead, he spent that week in the hospital, sitting by Jacob's bedside, holding him, feeding him and watching the nurses suction his throat.

When the week ended, we quickly developed a new routine: we left our house together and he walked to his office a short distance from our home. I got into my car for the twenty-minute drive to the hospital. As I was heading downtown, my heart would start beating faster. I was easily annoyed by slow-moving cars. I wanted to roll down my window and scream at them, "Hurry up, I have to get to the hospital!" I purposely left the house early, trying to avoid the nasty rush-hour traffic. And I arrived at HSC before the night shift nurse left, able to hear firsthand how Jacob was while I wasn't there.

At the end of the day, Andrew took the subway down to the hospital and met us in Jacob's room. Together, and sometimes with Jacob in tow, we took the elevator down to the cafeteria to have dinner. Once in a while friends or family members would join us, sometimes even bringing us a meal.

My husband remarked, on more than one occasion, how unfair it was that I was glued to Jacob's side while he had a chance to lose himself in his work for many hours during the day.

Unfair, indeed, but this was our new reality.

• • •

Early in our three-month stay, a doctor from the genetics department approached me. Would I mind answering some questions about my family history? Jacob's team of doctors wanted to investigate whether his mysterious symptoms, most notably bilateral vocal cord paralysis, were caused by a genetic disorder.

The doctor, a young man at the start of his career, had a pleasant manner and explained that we would probably never receive a definitive diagnosis. He also stated that I should hope he didn't find one. In my foggy post-birth brain, I didn't realize what he was telling me. It took a long time for me to understand that a genetic disease is a horrible diagnosis, one with no cure.

I answered all his questions, from "are Andrew and I related?" (we are not) to queries about the details of my grandmother's children's births. I told him that my grandmother had two sons who died in infancy in Montreal in the 1940s. Her first child died shortly after birth with a malformed larynx, and she was told that her second son's death at twenty-two months was the result of a birth injury. My mother, the middle baby, was her only child who survived. This information was noted in what was quickly becoming Jacob's large medical file and that was it. There was no follow-up scheduled, which was not surprising given that so many specialists were reviewing my son's unusual symptoms.

I thought about how quickly my life had changed. For the past six months, I had eagerly devoured all the pregnancy and parenting books I could find. I sat on my couch, one arm resting on my growing belly, the other holding a book that compared the merits of different brands and models of infant paraphernalia, from strollers to cribs to car seats. I spent countless hours fretting over whether the baby's room should have a white or beige crib. I even test-drove strollers, pushing three different models up and down the pavement behind the store.

That period of my life was full of possibilities. I had a few friends with whom to share the latest research on infant development, help select a pediatrician, and decide on which neighbourhoods would be the best to raise our kids. And then Jacob was born, and all of these well-thought-out plans became irrelevant.

• • •

At nine days old, we agreed to allow Jacob to have an MRI. The test would enable the doctors to see the inside of his brain, and except for the general anesthetic required for sedation, it was safe and painless. Shortly before Jacob was wheeled into the MRI tube, Dr. Forte tried to reassure us. "Don't worry," he said. "We don't expect to find anything."

So, we tried our best to stay calm, not expecting any unusual information.

About forty-five minutes later, a doctor came to us and explained that they were taking Jacob for a CT scan because they wanted to double-check something they had seen on the MRI. Again, we were told not to worry and we waited for the results that were expected later that afternoon.

Our parents were with us and we chatted about insignificant things. We tried our best to pass the time while watching the hallways for any sign of Jacob or the doctors who had whisked him away.

Jacob was wheeled back to his spot in the NICU about an hour later, still intubated and sedated. The doctors said he had been fine during the procedures and would rouse shortly. We were also informed that the results would be available at 3 p.m., at which time the doctor in charge of the NICU would review them with us. Although no specific information was shared, we knew something wasn't right. Jacob had had to wait a few days until the doctors were able to book the MRI because of high demand and long waiting lists, but immediately following the test, my son was taken for an unscheduled procedure. After nine days of hospital living, I knew that something serious was going on if they were able to get a CT performed without a pre-booked appointment. The tests had uncovered an unexpected complication.

At the appointed time, Andrew and I accompanied the physician into a meeting room where he pulled up Jacob's images on the computer screen. He explained that the MRI showed a problem with Jacob's myelin, the insulation that encases every nerve in our bodies. He stated that the true extent of Jacob's troubles would not be known for some time, but we were looking at a possible diagnosis of Cerebral Palsy. It would take about a year until they could be certain.

This doctor was so patient with us. I remember him going over and over the same information. I felt like I was seeing my own brain with broken parts on the screen. I was having trouble comprehending the information, probably because it was so disheartening and also because it was unexpected. I saw the doctor's lips move, knew words were coming out of his mouth, but I couldn't process what he was saying. This was supposed to be a simple, routine test. The results came as a sucker punch. More than one doctor had told us that they were not expecting to find anything unusual on the MRI and, like a fool, I believed them.

The horror of this finding started to sink in when Andrew and I walked back into the NICU waiting room. As I entered, I saw our whole family: my parents and Andrew's, but also his three siblings and their spouses. My mother-in-law had called her children to tell them we were receiving some devastating news and asked if they could come to the hospital. When she heard that there was an unscheduled CT scan being performed, she must have realized that something terrible had been found on the tests. This was the middle of the day, and seeing our family—who had all dropped their work commitments to share in our grief—made the news more real to me. My heart still hurts when I picture their sympathetic faces in the waiting room on the afternoon that Jacob was nine days old.

As horrible as the test results were, the new information did not change Jacob's care plan. The staff still tried to ensure that his airway remained clear, that he was able to digest the milk that dripped into his stomach and that he gained weight. The goal was to stabilize his symptoms so he could come home.

About three weeks after Jacob was born, he was moved out of the NICU to a room on the 7th floor, close to the nurses' station. The unit was organized so that almost all of the kids (most were over the age of four) had their own room, complete with an uncomfortable vinyl bench that could double as a bed. The nurses tried to assure us that Jacob would be well looked after and that we didn't need to stay overnight. They said their high nurse-to-patient ratio ensured that someone would be available should Jacob begin to cry. As much as I wanted to believe them, I couldn't. And I started to realize that the more sleep-deprived I became, the less coherent I was.

Unlike mothers of healthy infants, I couldn't nap while my baby napped. There was too much going on at the hospital. And I didn't get much sleep at home, despite Jacob not waking me. Because Jacob was having so much trouble gaining weight and breast milk is known to be the easiest food to digest, I was expressing my milk seven times a day, every three to four hours around the clock, with the hope that the benefits of breast milk would help make him stronger.

Before Jacob's birth, we'd arranged for a woman to help us at home with our newborn. Her role was to tend to my child's needs during the night, bringing him to me for a feeding and then putting him back to sleep. Now, instead of coming to our house, she came to the hospital and stayed overnight with Jacob in his room. Knowing that my little guy wasn't alone overnight, and that someone was there to summon a nurse when needed, enabled me to get the sleep I so desperately required in order to care for him during the day.

Shortly before Jake was six weeks old, his medical team felt he was ready to be discharged. But Andrew and I were not convinced that we would be able to care for him outside the hospital walls. Although we were gaining confidence in our abilities to look after him, we both depended too strongly on the proximity of the nurses when something unexpected happened, or when we were unsure of what to do.

The doctors suggested a compromise to which we reluctantly agreed: we would take our son home, but the hospital would save his room for twenty-four hours in case we needed to return.

I packed up Jacob's clothes, his red bear, and the few toys we'd collected from friends who had stopped by to visit. Together, our little family of three left the hospital with a lot of trepidation. I had a gnawing feeling in my gut that this was not a good idea. The doctors had been willing to discharge Jacob at two days old when he clearly wasn't ready. Six weeks later, I still didn't believe that my son was out of danger. We hesitantly drove away, scared to start this new phase of independent parenting, the skilled support team staying behind.

•   •   •

The first day and night were okay. Jacob didn't seem to notice his new surroundings and we had a nurse who cared for him during the night, attending to his feeding, medication and overall safety. Closing in on the twenty-four hour window, I called Jacob's doctor at HSC. I was still not convinced we were out of danger so I pleaded with him to save Jake's room for one more day. I let out a great sigh of relief when he agreed. Even though I tried to stifle it, he must have heard the fear in my voice.

As the sun set on that day, Jacob became restless. His breathing was laboured, more so than usual, and his indrawing was more pronounced. Andrew and I took turns suctioning the mucus from his airway but we couldn't quiet his noisy inhalations. Trying to stay calm but teetering on the edge of full-blown panic, we debated calling 911. We decided to phone our brother-in-law instead. David is an Ear, Nose, and Throat physician and was familiar with Jacob's short and complicated history.

About fifteen minutes later, David arrived and started suctioning his nephew to no avail. Nothing he tried seemed to relieve Jacob's suffering for more than a brief moment or two. David turned, faced us and stated that Jacob was too ill to be at home. And so, in the very late hours of the day, we decided to bring him back to his reserved room at HSC.

A few days later, on June 24, the purchase of our first house closed. This milestone event was overshadowed by more important things, like the issue of why our baby couldn't breathe properly. What we had expected to be an exciting experience turned out to be an inconvenience. I wouldn't leave the hospital, so Andrew arranged to have the documents brought to Jacob's room. The papers were signed and the house was ours.

The things I had been looking forward to doing once we were home owners became no more than a series of decisions that had to be made. There was no joy in the process of preparing our new house. Paint colours were chosen in a matter of minutes under the fluorescent lights in Jacob's beige hospital room. Before he was born, I would have struggled over this decision, convinced that each choice had to be perfect. After Jacob's birth, it was just paint.

Looking back at the way I'd agonized over selecting the perfect bedding for Jacob's crib, I cringed. I thought about how innocent and utterly clueless I had been, believing that the colour of Jacob's car seat really mattered. I now realize how trivial it was.

• • •

When Jacob was six weeks old, the doctors approached us about having a hole surgically cut into his stomach so a tube could directly administer his nutrition which was a more permanent solution than the NG tube. It took me a few days to consent to the gastrostomy tube (G-tube) surgery. I was having trouble accepting that my son would require a tube to eat for the rest of his life.

I had not yet gotten comfortable with the process of setting up Jake's NG feed. Before any food was administered, we had to ensure that the tube did not dislodge from his stomach. If it moved up into his lungs and the food was discharged there, he could drown. In order to check the placement, we had to insert air into the tube while listening with a stethoscope for a "pop" sound in his stomach. It was a subtle noise, and with Jake's loud, congested breathing, I was never sure if I was doing it properly. I always wanted a nurse to double-check before I started a feed. The risk was too great. The G-tube would definitely be safer.

But the NG tube was a *temporary* way to feed my son. To me, it meant that he would one day be able to graduate to eating like everyone else. Consenting to the surgery meant accepting that this was not likely to happen—Jacob would never learn to eat by his mouth. But the doctors wouldn't say this. They couched their remarks in sentences like, "Just because he has a G-tube doesn't mean you can't keep trying to feed him."

Part of the campaign to have me agree to the procedure involved the nurses taking me down the hall to the room of a little girl who had just had the surgery. They wanted me to see what a G-tube looked like and observe a feeding. The nurses reasoned that it would seem less scary if I saw the reality instead of just trying to visualize it. I still remember the red-haired girl, about nine years old, lying motionless on her bed while food dripped into her stomach. She was in the late stages of a disease whose only similarity to Jacob's was that they both lacked the ability to eat by mouth. I saw the tube and understood how it worked. But I couldn't tear my eyes away from this little girl's blank face. She was awake but made no indication that I was in the room or conversing with her mother. She did not react when her mother lifted her hospital gown to show me what her stomach looked like with the new tube. I remember being thankful that Jacob did not share her disease.

Seeing an actual G-tube helped and, ironically, so did having an inexperienced nurse assigned to Jacob a few nights later. Andrew and I were getting ready to leave for the evening when the nurse came into Jacob's room to start setting up his 8 p.m. feed. As per protocol, she put the stethoscope to his stomach and listened for the "pop" sound and did not hear it. She was convinced the feeding tube was dislodged and needed to be replaced. One nurse restrained my son while the other one pulled out the NG tube and reinserted a new one, threading it up his nose until it turned and went down his throat, eventually ending in his little stomach. As expected, my son was upset, screaming and scared throughout this procedure. Over an hour had elapsed since the nurse arrived to set up his feed and Jake was likely hungry on top of everything else. After a bit of suctioning by the nurse, his feed was in place. It didn't take long for Jacob to fall asleep, likely worn out by the trauma of the NG tube change.

When I leaned in to kiss my baby goodnight, I noticed that the feed was flowing freely into his tube at an alarming rate. Instead of the usual one drip per second, the nurse had inadvertently opened the toggle so the milk flowed at a rate similar to an open water tap. I was enraged at her incompetence, especially since I did not believe the tube had dislodged in the first place. I was terrified that the incidents of the evening would weaken my son and cause him additional problems. Luckily, he did not seem to suffer any adverse consequences, short of the pain associated with the tube change. But before leaving for the evening, I submitted a request that was immediately granted. Only nurses with significant experience would be assigned to care for my son.

Eventually Andrew and I relented and signed the consent forms for the surgery. We also asked about the possibility of having Jacob circumcised while he was under general anesthetic. He was too fragile to have a regular bris ceremony at the prescribed eight days of life, and by six weeks old it is deemed too painful a procedure to perform without an anesthetic. In a wonderful stroke of luck, the head of surgery at HSC was also a *mohel*, a man qualified by Jewish law to perform this religious rite of passage.

Shortly before his stomach was cut for his G-tube, Jacob had his bris under the glaring lights of the operating room, without his family present. But one consolation was that Jacob was wearing my grandfather's, his namesake's, kippa on his head while the bris was conducted and the blessings recited. It wasn't the way I'd envisioned this momentous event, but at least it was completed, safely and painlessly.

When I saw Jacob post-surgery I barely recognized my little guy! Since his second full day of life, a giant bandage had covered half his face. Walking over to his crib, I saw an adorable little baby with a full head of dark brown hair and pudgy cheeks. Two of them. This new ability to see my son—all of him!—was the first positive thing about the surgery. I could kiss both sides of his face now and feel his warm cheeks.

Once the permanent tube was in place, I knew I had to learn how to feed him by myself. I became proficient in how to control the speed of the drips to make sure the milk didn't flow too quickly. I had plenty of practice as this process was repeated every three hours, around the clock. And it was scary. I had to remember which way to move the toggle—one way to increase and the other to slow the flow. Each time Jacob would choke or vomit, which happened several times during a feed, the switch needed to be turned off. With trembling hands, I'd fumble the toggle, terrified I'd open the flow instead of closing it off. Eventually, I got used to it. Like typing my name on a keyboard, adjusting the flow was something my hands were eventually able to do without looking. This procedure took a long time—it required nearly an hour for the milk to drip into his body, longer if he was crying or choking. We had to hold him still, virtually motionless, for an hour post-feed to reduce the likelihood of vomiting.

Being a mother took on a new meaning for me. Yes, I held my son like any new mother, but it was different. Nothing was the way I'd thought it would be. I had to make sure I did not dislodge any of the tubes that helped him live. Yes, I fed my son like any new mother, but it was different. Instead of holding him to my breast or placing a bottle in his mouth, I had to connect him to a feeding system that dripped pumped breast milk into a tube that was surgically inserted into his stomach, bypassing his mouth. And yes, eventually I was allowed to take him for walks in his stroller, but that was different too. We walked in the halls of the hospital, stopping occasionally so I could place a suction tube in his mouth to help him breathe.

As we were given the freedom to venture farther away from his room, I gained confidence in my ability to feed Jake by myself and overcame my revulsion at threading a tube up his nose and down his throat for the deep suctioning he sometimes required. But I was still terrified. I can still remember feeling my inexperienced hands trembling as I snaked the tube into his nose until it reached the point where it would turn, move down his throat and clear the thick mucous that was impeding his airway. I was not enjoying this part of motherhood. Not one bit.

But I learned how to take care of my son. I received intense, on-the-job medical training by the nurses during Jake's three-month hospital stay. All my education was from the trained professionals I encountered daily at the hospital. They were wonderful and supportive and caring, but I felt isolated—I didn't know anyone who had a child like mine, one who struggled each day to breathe, to move, to grow. In so many ways, I was alone.

"Courage is being scared to death –
and saddling up anyway!"

John Wayne

CHAPTER 3

COMING HOME

At almost three months old, Jacob had not achieved any of the typical infant milestones. He didn't smile, made no attempt to hold his head up, kick his legs or put his hands in his mouth. He didn't babble and the only sounds he made were crying and screaming. I want to believe he knew me—I was always by his side and was often able to quiet his screams—although I can't be sure.

We began discussing the possibility of discharging him from the hospital so that he could finally come home. This wasn't the first time we'd entertained this idea, but we hoped that this time it would actually happen.

As painful as it was to see my baby in the hospital, I was too frightened to think about him living at home. The next time Jacob's doctor broached the idea, I panicked. I said I wasn't capable of managing on my own and that he was safer in the hospital surrounded by nurses. The topic was dropped for a few days.

The third time the doctor recommended a discharge, I refused. I said I wasn't ready. I was told that if I didn't want to bring him home, we'd need to consider an alternative placement. He suggested a long-term care hospital where Jacob could live, without us.

My grandmother placed her son in a "home" in the 1940s. Thirty years later, my cousin Audrey did the same for her seriously ill son. Neither regretted her decision and it allowed them to move on and build a "normal" life, one that resembled that of their friends. But I adamantly refused to consider this option. I simply wouldn't do it. Although I respected their decisions, I felt like I would be abandoning my baby. I wasn't ready to make a choice, but I was being forced to do so nonetheless. The only thing I knew for certain was that I wouldn't consider placing him in a long-term care facility.

The wheels were put in motion to bring Jacob home.

The hospital staff suggested that Andrew and I get certified in CPR. One of the discharge nurses arranged for an instructor to spend several hours with us in an office down the hall from Jacob's room. It had been decades since I'd first learned mouth-to-mouth resucitation—I was taught it in swimming class when I was a child. The stakes were different here. I wasn't learning it to get a badge and proceed to the next level. I paid close attention to each concept that was explained, absorbing the details I'd need to save my son's life in case he stopped breathing at home. It was vital that I remember every single word the instructor said.

The next step in preparation for Jacob's discharge was an assessment by the Community Care Access Centre (CCAC), the provincially funded group that provides access to health care in the home. Without knocking, a mature-looking stocky woman walked into Jacob's room and announced that she was from the CCAC and was going to determine how much home care he would receive. She stood at his bedside, peering over the side rails, and asked a few questions, such as whether I was Jacob's mother and what treatment he was receiving.

A few minutes later, when she finished writing the notes in her file, she looked up at me and said that Jacob did not qualify for any assistance because "his case was not complex enough." My body started trembling, partially out of anger and partially out of fear. I wanted to pounce on her and watch my nails leave bloody marks on her wrinkled face while screaming every bad word I knew. Fortunately for her, a nurse who was present quickly came to my side and tried to calm me down. I was in tears as the CCAC representative walked out of the room. I simply could not understand how this insensitive woman could look me in the eye and state that my son, whose breathing was as loud as the beeping of the monitors he still wore, did not qualify as a "complex" case. As the nurse tried to reassure me, I kept repeating that I couldn't take him home, not without nursing support.

Doctors are notoriously late for appointments. Jacob and I experienced that daily. I learned to differentiate between what I called "real time" and "hospital time." If we had a test scheduled for 11 a.m. in real time, it would be around 2 p.m. before he was seen. Strangely, this didn't bother me all that much—we didn't have anywhere else to be, and we just got used to it. But when the CCAC debacle occurred, the doctors moved faster than I'd seen them move in the entire three months Jacob had been an in-patient.

Jacob's medical team were appalled by the woman's assessment and wondered aloud why she had treated us so poorly. They tossed around some speculations, but the only thing that really mattered was fixing the mistake that had been made. The staff on Jacob's floor believed that my son's symptoms qualified him as one of the most complex cases they had treated in years. When the doctor called the CCAC to start an appeal process, he mentioned that fact. Within twenty-four hours, an appeal was submitted and a reassessment occurred. In this situation, it turned out, hospital time was just as fast as real time, and for that I was grateful.

When Jacob was reassessed by a second CCAC representative, he qualified for the maximum number of government-funded nursing hours because of the complexity and severity of his undi-agnosed condition. The new CCAC delegate apologized for her col-league's error and could not explain why we had been mistreated.

I was comforted by the knowledge that when we came home, Jacob would have a registered nurse caring for him overnight so that I could sleep—or at least try to sleep—and be prepared to resume his care in the morning.

With each day that passed, it seemed we were getting closer to being discharged. Each outstanding item was addressed and the lengthy to-do list was nearly complete.

Before we were allowed to leave the safety of the hospital, all the medical supplies we needed to care for Jacob were ordered by the discharge planner and delivered to our house. It was a much more thorough discharge than the one that had taken place when Jacob was six weeks old. The medical team wanted to ensure that all the arrangements were in place before we brought Jacob home. Jacob was the only one in the unit who had been hospitalized for such a lengthy period (most kids were in for a day or two), so the staff were well versed in his care. They were doing everything they could to ensure we were properly equipped to care for our son. Eight brown boxes of various sizes containing tubing, bottles, syringes, suction catheters in different sizes, medical tape, adhesive removal and two IV poles littered the main floor of our home.

I reluctantly accepted the fact that I required help to care for my son. Andrew, my parents, my in-laws and Jake's doctors spent a lot of time convincing me that I couldn't do it alone. They weren't trying to sabotage my efforts, they were simply able to acknowledge something that I didn't want to admit. His medical needs were com-plex and he required intense supervision. It was impossible for me to manage Jacob's care by myself and many people made sure I understood this.

With the assistance of the nurses and doctors at HSC, Jacob's caregivers were put in place. I didn't love the idea that strangers would be in my house in the wee hours of the night, free to roam around and investigate whatever looked interesting to them. Conversely, the thought of having an attentive nurse beside Jacob's crib during the long, dark hours helped calm my jittery mind. The nurse's role was to remain alert, and to provide medication and tube feeding at predetermined hours. Due to his paralyzed vocal cords, Jacob vomited frequently and was at constant risk of aspiration. His life would literally depend on the vigilance of the nurses' care. Eventually, the knowledge that there would be a skilled nurse caring for Jacob when I could not overcame the ambiguity I felt about having a stranger in my house.

• • •

It was late morning on July 22 by the time we arrived at home with Jacob. I carried him from the car to the house and took a deep breath before we entered. This is it, I thought. We're here to stay. I was scared but excited. My baby was finally home.

I talked to Jacob as we walked through the door, telling him where we were. I toured him around the main floor and then brought him upstairs to see his bedroom. I pointed to the pale blue walls and showed him the natural wood-coloured crib I'd painstakingly selected months before his birth. I placed his red bear at the foot of his new bed, in the same place it had been in the hospital.

Obviously, Jacob didn't understand a word I was saying, but it felt right to introduce him to his new home in this way. I sat in the rocking chair and held him in my arms as Andrew set up his first feed at home.

When the meal was ready, I brought Jacob downstairs and positioned myself on the sofa, preparing to sit motionless for the next two hours while my baby was fed and trying to digest the food without vomiting. At least I would be sitting on my sofa instead of the hard chair in the hospital, I reasoned.

As I watched him sleep and the milk drip into his belly, I started to relax. Maybe being home was a good thing, maybe it would be okay. I wouldn't have to rush down to the hospital every morning and feel my heart race as I approached his room. I wouldn't have to wonder if I would get an emergency phone call during the night telling me that something terrible had happened to my son. My baby was home, exactly where he should be.

• • •

By that evening, I was exhausted beyond belief; it had been an emotionally draining day. All the planning and preparing was over and my son was home, safely asleep in his new bed. Andrew and I took turns watching him sleep while we waited for the night nurse to arrive.

As arranged by the discharge planner at HSC, a nurse arrived at our door at precisely 11:30 p.m. When the doorbell rang, Andrew answered it and escorted her upstairs. After introducing myself, I brought her over to Jacob's crib and introduced her to my baby, her patient. We showed her where all Jake's supplies were located and reviewed his feeding schedule, his medications and how we set up the feed. We reiterated that Jacob's vocal cords were paralyzed and that he was at constant risk of choking. We reminded her that it was imperative that she remain awake and alert throughout the night. The nurse listened attentively and reassured us that she was comfortable and capable in her role. Andrew and I left her alone with our son while we attempted to sleep in our room down the hall.

I remember thinking how bizarre this process was—a stranger, sent by an administrator at a nursing agency, would be responsible for my son's safety. I didn't know anything about this nurse: what her previous job experience was, whether her previous patients liked her. I wasn't given the opportunity to interview her or check her references. I was forced to rely on the agency's screening process, and I didn't have any clue how thorough it was. But my only other option was to refuse the government-funded nurse and try to find and pay for one myself. There really wasn't a choice at all.

A few hours later, around 2:30 a.m., I decided to peek in on my baby and see how his night was progressing. I was shocked to find the nurse asleep in the rocking chair, my fragile son napping in her arms. I wanted to run over and grab Jacob. I loudly called her name, three times, before she roused from her slumber. Trying to stay calm, I asked her to please return my son to his crib. I explained again why it was so important for her to stay awake during her shift. I implored her to stay alert and monitor him for any signs of distress.

I hesitantly returned to my bedroom. Lying in bed, my mind was racing, replaying the scene I had walked in on earlier in Jake's room. I forced myself to stay where I was because I knew I needed to sleep, but my mind wouldn't slow down enough to let me. A few hours later, I re-entered my son's room only to find the nurse, again, fast asleep in the chair.

The next morning I called the agency to report the unprofessional behaviour of the nurse they had assigned to look after Jacob. I naively assumed that the agency's supervisor would realize the danger my son was in, profusely apologize and assign a more trustworthy nurse to his care. But the response I received angered and frustrated me. I was informed that she was the only nurse available at the moment and we would either have to accept her or not have a nurse until they could hire and train someone else.

I didn't know what to do. I called the Discharge Planner at HSC and recounted what happened. Our options were limited. We had to take the sleeping nurse back until a new one could be assigned to Jacob's care.

The first week was hard. The whole point of having a night nurse care for Jacob was so that I could rest and be ready for the intense care that I would provide during the day. With a nurse we couldn't trust, it was hard for me to sleep and I found myself popping into his room numerous times during the night.

After six virtually sleepless nights, the agency called to say they'd hired a new nurse who they believed would be better suited to caring for our son. Her name was Emily and on her first night, she was actually awake each time I entered Jake's room to check. As the nights wore on, my trust grew and I began to believe that Jacob was in good hands.

We settled into a pattern. Emily was Jacob's night nurse from Monday to Friday; the weekends were still uncertain. Most of the nurses we worked with were compassionate people, but that was not the only qualification necessary for caring for my son. I can still feel my eyes bulging in horror when I watched a nurse administer Jacob's medication into the air, missing his feeding tube by a few inches. When I asked her what she was doing, she replied that she couldn't see the opening of his tube. It turned out that her vision problems were so severe that her driver's license had been revoked. The agency insisted she was capable of caring for my child when clearly, she was not.

I've mistakenly assumed that a nurse would be able to know when a thermometer registers a fever. Jacob has been given Tylenol when his temperature was 97.8 Fahrenheit because a nurse has forgotten that normal is 98.6. I've also assumed that a nurse would be able to differentiate between ¼ and ½ tablet. I was wrong and Jacob received the incorrect dose of medication countless times.

I will never forget when I was out pushing my infant twins in a stroller, enjoying the warm spring afternoon when my cell phone rang. "This is the police. We have your son, please come and get him." It took me a few moments to comprehend what the officer was telling me but as soon as I did, I sprang into action. I ran back home, dropped my twins off with my parents, jumped into my car and sped off to retrieve Jacob from Winner's.

As I entered the store, I was escorted to a windowless room where Jacob was waiting, watched by a police officer and store employee. Our nurse was arrested for shoplifting, hiding items behind my three-year-old son's back.

At one point over the years, I thought I found my "Mary Poppins." Like Julie Andrews in the movie, Krystal swooped in and immediately took charge. She made the job seem effortless and Jacob loved her. She devised creative games and introduced him to the music on her MP3 player. She organized his medical supplies and notified me when I needed to reorder any inventory. I started to relax more than I had in years knowing that Jacob was in such capable hands. But, sadly for us, she moved back home to Saskatchewan after six short months with us.

•   •   •

It would take several years before a stable schedule was formed and we felt that our nights were safely covered by competent and reliable nurses—several years before I was able to get a decent night's sleep so that I had the physical and emotional stamina to cope with the daily stresses of mothering my very ill child whose rare symptoms didn't fit into any identified disorder ... Yet.

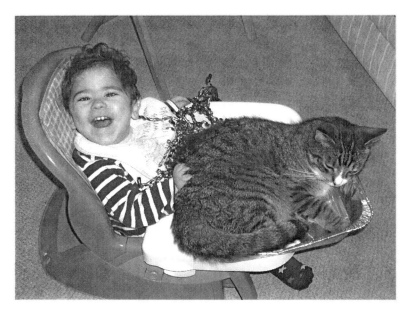

Jacob and Spot, his favourite cat

— NOVEMBER 23, 2003 —

"Do not let the behaviour of others destroy your inner peace."

Dalai Lama

CHAPTER 4

THE ARTICLE THAT
CHANGED EVERYTHING

When Jacob was still in the hospital, the question I asked each and every physician who examined him was the same: Do you know what is wrong with my son? Unfortunately, I was no closer to getting an answer when Jacob was finally discharged than I was on the day he was born.

On several occasions, Andrew and I were informed that it was probably a random occurrence that Jacob was not well and that the true extent of his challenges would only become clear as he aged. I asked how we were supposed to live with the uncertainty. How were we to move forward if Jake needed to be older before they could start trying to figure things out? The doctors simply shrugged and said there was nothing else they could do. I watched their backs as they walked out of the room and into the neighbouring one. It was as if my son's struggles left their thoughts as soon as they crossed the threshold.

The one thing all of the medical professionals seemed to agree on was that if we chose to have more children, it was unlikely they would be affected with Jacob's mysterious illness. Apparently, the likelihood of having a child with special needs is four per cent for the general population and "only" an additional three per cent for parents who already have a child with challenges. Their assurances didn't make any sense to me. The more I thought about it, the angrier I became. I had been told, repeatedly and by different doctors, that Jacob didn't have a diagnosis. Even the specialists didn't know what was wrong with him. But if they didn't know what he had, how could they tell me so certainly that the odds of having another sick child were only slightly higher than they would have been if I didn't have Jacob? It was ludicrous.

Even at the time, Andrew and I believed that these doctors were wrong. But it wasn't until later that we learned how grossly off the mark they were.

I hated that no one was giving us anything to go on, that no one seemed willing to get to the bottom of Jacob's problems. Of course, the doctors examined Jacob and spoke to us. We talked about how to treat his constant vomiting and what type of suctioning he required, but I knew that I needed to find someone who cared, someone who saw Jacob as more than simply a patient to be managed. I had to find a way to ensure that my son's severe and strange symptoms stayed in a doctor's mind long after the exam was over. I wanted someone to take the time to think about my son, to research his symptoms, to brainstorm with various specialists and make it his or her mission to find a diagnosis. Living in limbo simply wasn't an option for me.

I knew I wouldn't be able to move forward without knowing what was wrong, so I resolved to do everything and anything to track down the cause of Jacob's medical issues. I wanted to know what was wrong with him and I believed that once I had a diagnosis, I would be able to focus on getting him better. Until I knew the root cause of his symptoms, all I could do was treat each issue as it arose. It wasn't enough. I had to be proactive; Jacob's life depended on it.

I grappled with these thoughts each and every day, but in the meantime, life went on. I enjoyed having Jacob home and we quickly settled into our new routine. I hadn't realized how tiring it was shuffling back and forth to the hospital each day until I didn't have to do it anymore. Life wasn't quiet, but it was so much better than when he'd been too unstable to come home.

One day, I realized that I had changed. Somehow along the way, in the midst of all the feedings, appointments and isolation, I had stopped saying that I couldn't handle it. I had stopped feeling like I was going to scream every time we were told that there was nothing anyone could do. I'd stopped shaking every time I had to suction Jacob and I'd stopped apologizing to strangers in waiting rooms for his screaming.

While I was happy with my new outlook, there were still difficult moments. Although I had come to accept that Jacob's problems were ongoing and incredibly serious, I continued to struggle with the differences between my former expectations and my new reality. This was not the way I had visualized motherhood. Seeing a healthy child was so painful for me that I often felt like I was going to collapse in tears. When I saw a baby that was the same age as Jacob, I had to look away. I couldn't help but think that my son should be sitting like that by now, that he should be able to smile too. When I overheard a mother complain about her child needing glasses, I wanted to scream at her to be thankful for having a child that could walk and talk.

Once, when a friend and I were out for a walk with our babies, hers several months older than Jacob, I listened quietly as she said, "It's been such a terrible day. He's been so cranky." On the outside, I smiled and nodded, but inside I was stunned. I couldn't believe what she was complaining about, or that she was complaining about it to me—as if I, of all people, would understand. I had to fight the urge to say, "You've got to be kidding. I would change places with you in a second if my biggest worry was how awful my son feels as a result of his twelve-month immunization." I wanted to grab her by her shoulders, look her straight in the eyes and scream the words that were forming in my head: "Try living with a medically fragile infant who suffers excruciating pain every time a drop of milk or life-sustaining medication is put directly into his stomach through a surgically implanted tube. How can you be so insensitive as to think I could share your grief over a simple pinprick in his arm?"

But I bit my tongue. I focused on transferring my sleeping curly-haired baby from his stroller to the house. I knew that my friend hadn't meant to be insensitive—in fact, I was pretty sure she'd have been mortified if I'd called it to her attention. Still, my feelings were deeply hurt. For the sake of our friendship, I made a mental note not to take our kids for a walk together again. I wasn't sure I would be able to muster the same restraint twice.

I wrestled with two conflicting desires. On the one hand, I wanted to isolate myself so that I wouldn't have to see what "normal" families looked like. On the other, I craved some semblance of normal adult contact with non-doctors. My first choice was to stay home—it took too much energy to get dressed and force myself to concentrate on conversation—but on the occasions when I was coaxed out, my preference was to socialize with friends without their children. I didn't want to hear about their kids' achievements. I was at my strongest when I could block out all the bad and scary things I was living through with my child.

If Jacob had been born healthy, I probably would have been able to empathize with my friends' concerns. But he wasn't and I couldn't. I wondered if I would ever be able to relate to my friends' daily challenges, or if having a severely disabled child had changed me so much that I would never be able to fathom their typical, everyday concerns.

Listening to friends' stories about their kids felt like a red-hot knife slicing through my heart. On the rare occasions when Jake and I went out for a walk, I avoided any route that led us past a park for fear of watching other kids playing. On the odd times when I would allow my parents to drag me out of the house to a neighbourhood eatery, it was on the condition that we would not be seated in the back of the restaurant, where all the parents and kids were placed. I couldn't help but stare at other toddlers, thinking how amazing it would be if Jacob could hold a spoon and bang it on the table.

• • •

One of the ways I learned to cope with Jacob and his medical issues was by throwing myself into researching a diagnosis. With no doctor to spearhead this quest, I spent hours scouring the Internet and medical journals for clues that might explain Jacob's assortment of symptoms. While my son slept, I read every article I could find on paralyzed vocal cords, stridor, reflux, swallowing difficulties and projectile vomiting in children. I amassed stacks of articles that measured over two feet high and contacted specialists all over the world with the hopes of finding someone with answers.

I felt good doing this. I believed I was helping my son; I was certainly doing more than his doctors, who were only medicating his symptoms to the best of their abilities. And the drugs they were giving him didn't seem to help. He was in constant pain, screaming incessantly and he was not gaining weight. It seemed like he was vomiting more than he was ingesting. We were at various doctor and therapy appointments at least four times a week and nothing was making him feel better.

I wasn't willing to accept a diagnosis of "unknown origin." I promised myself and my son that I wouldn't stop searching until I had a definitive answer. Little did I know that in the process, I would open a Pandora's box—one that never should have been closed in the first place.

It started when I decided that I wanted to learn more about my mother's brothers—my grandmother's children who had died in infancy. I wondered if their history would help shed some light on my son's condition. With no small amount of trepidation, I asked my grandmother if she would mind if I inquired as to whether her sons' hospital files existed. I was concerned about upsetting her; we seldom spoke about the tragedies she had lived through. I needn't have worried. She was eager to help, and immediately gave me her approval to start investigating.

With Gram's assistance, I accessed her sons' medical files from the Royal Victoria Hospital in Montreal. My skin tingled and my hands trembled as I read about the medical struggles that my son shared with my two deceased uncles. All three boys had strange-sounding, noisy breathing, in-drawing of their ribcages, nystagmus (jumpy, irregular eye movements), swallowing difficulties and severe vomiting.

In my inexperience and eagerness to find an answer, the symptoms sounded identical. To me, it was clear that these three boys shared the same disorder. I reviewed the documents with some of

Jake's doctors, who quickly and unanimously dismissed my comments and said there was nothing in the files that was relevant to Jacob's condition. They barely glanced at the pages, probably thinking that an untrained professional was unlikely to uncover anything significant since they were still stumped. I was astounded that they, with their experience and education, did not see what was so evident to me.

Determined to find information that could help Jacob, I began asking my parents and grandmother detailed questions about my extended family's medical history. I was told that my mother's cousin, Audrey, had a son, Corey, who was born in 1970 with encephalitis. More than ten years later, Audrey had moved from Montreal to Israel and had two sons and two daughters with a different husband. Her youngest son was sick.

Desperate to learn more about her children's health struggles, I called Audrey. She explained that Corey had been born with a breathing problem and was placed in an institution when he was nine months old. His care was simply too difficult for her to manage at home. She moved to Israel a few years later and never saw him again. He died when he was twelve years old, though she was not sure of the exact cause of his death. Audrey told me that she didn't see many common symptoms between Corey and Yochai, her fifth child, who was also affected with an undiagnosed medical condition. Believing that her two sons' challenges were unrelated but willing to help me investigate Jacob's situation, she provided me with the documents I required to access Corey's medical files.

A few weeks later, a white envelope arrived in the mail from the Montreal Children's Hospital. I opened it and read about the cousin I'd never met. My heart raced as familiar words jumped out at me:

"stridor," "crowing," "reflux," "inability to swallow," the same words that were constantly tossed around in reference to Jacob. More than ever, I was convinced that these boys in my family shared an unusual disorder.

I shared these notes during a meeting a few days later at the Hospital for Sick Children with Dr. Annette Feigenbaum, a geneticist, and Stacy Hewson, a genetic counsellor. Together we reviewed the historical records of my uncles, cousin and son. Everyone agreed that these boys appeared to share symptoms, some of which, like paralyzed vocal cords, were extremely rare.

Finally, others were starting to notice what I had noticed—that Jacob's illness was not a random occurrence. There appeared to be an uncommon genetic disorder in my family history that affected male children.

The final piece that glued the puzzle together, while simultaneously destroying my belief that doctors always act in their patients' best interest, came at the end of the appointment that Monday afternoon. Stacy left the room to photocopy some of my files. After a few minutes, she poked her head in and asked for Dr. Feigenbaum's assistance. The doctor turned to us, shrugged her shoulders, and said, "I guess she needs some help with the photocopy machine." If that was all Stacy had wanted, my life would be very different today.

They were gone for a long time, so long that Andrew and I began to wonder what was causing the delay. We were anxious to go back home; Jacob had an occupational therapy appointment I didn't want to miss and our parking meter was almost expired. In retrospect, these seem like such insignificant concerns. We had no idea our world was about to be permanently changed—again.

After about a half hour, they returned to the room with very serious expressions on their faces. Dr. Feigenbaum apologized for the delay. She told me that when I had given her several medical articles I thought would be of interest following our previous meeting, she had passed them onto Stacy. One of the articles caught Stacy's eye and she wanted to learn more about the issue. She noticed the reference in the bibliography and retrieved it from the hospital's library. During the course of our meeting, as we'd reviewed the information in my files, Stacy was reminded of something she had read earlier. She shared this information with Dr. Feigenbaum while Andrew and I were waiting for them to return.

Dr. Feigenbaum handed me the article that Stacy had accessed from their library a few days earlier. It was from a medical journal, aptly titled "Clinical Genetics". As I reached out to take it from her, Dr. Feigenbaum said, "We think this is your family." I thought she meant that the article was about a family like mine. But that wasn't what she was saying at all.

The article, entitled "Familial Laryngeal Abductor Paralysis and Psychomotor Retardation," had been published in 1973. It described Corey and my uncles. It had photographs of Corey and an extended family tree. I was surprised to see sections in the article that were taken, verbatim, from the medical files I'd brought to the meeting. I crumpled to the floor, the article resting on the little table in front of me. I flipped through the pages, the words not registering in my mind. I kept returning to the family tree and the photographs of Corey with his huge eyes and expressionless face.

After what seemed like a long time, I realized that I was finally staring at the shocking truth: nearly thirty-five years earlier, Corey's doctors had concluded that my family has a genetic mutation. They didn't have a name for it at the time, but stated that it was carried by females, who have a fifty per cent chance of passing it to any off-spring. If a female child has this mutation, she will be a carrier, like me; if a male child has this defective gene, he will be sick, like Jacob.

I will never forget that moment in the doctor's office—the moment when I realized that I had unwittingly given my son a horrible disease. Even now, nine years later, the memory still causes my stomach to flip. I sat on the floor, Andrew in the chair next to me. The room was silent; Dr. Feigenbaum and Stacy were letting the information seep into our minds. I got up from the floor and walked over to the window at the other end of the room. My mind was reeling but everything around me felt frozen in time. I exhaled—I must have been holding my breath and my heart was pounding quickly in my chest. I spoke out loud the conclusions that everyone else in the room had already drawn: my uncle hadn't died of a birth injury; Corey didn't have encephalitis; and I was the cause of Jacob's medical struggles. As the pieces fell into place, I knew for certain that Jacob was not going to outgrow his issues.

As early as 1973, when I was merely five years old, two doctors—Gordon Watters and Naomi Fitch—had known about the genetic mutation that my family carried. Dr. Watters was Corey's neurologist and cared for him on several occasions over the course of Corey's short life. He examined him repeatedly and ordered a series of painful and invasive tests to prove his hypothesis. Drs. Watters and Fitch studied our family history, wrote about it, and had it published for the entire medical community to read. Somehow, they did not believe it was necessary to inform Audrey, my grandmother, or mother because they did not mention our family name. The doctors' irresponsible and self-serving actions gained them recognition in a prestigious medical publication but left innocent victims in their wake. For professionals whose motto is "first do no harm," they had failed miserably.

When I returned home that afternoon, I called my mother to tell her about the article. She was astounded, as was my grandmother. I emailed a copy of the article to Audrey and she said that she didn't recall the doctors, nor had she ever seen the photos of her son that were published. Since they were taken when Corey was in the institution, she had never given her consent.

The following day, I tried to locate the doctors. I couldn't trace Dr. Fitch but Dr. Gordon Watters was still working as a pediatric neurologist at the Montreal Children's Hospital. I phoned his office and left a message with his secretary. I told her that I believed I was related to a family he'd written about in the 1970s and was anxious to speak with him. I explained that I believed my son had the same disease he described in his paper.

When I didn't hear from him a few days later, I called back. I pleaded with the secretary to have her boss contact me. She said he was out of town but that she would fax him my information and ensure that he received the message. I was desperate to speak with Dr. Watters; I wanted to know if he had any information that could help Jacob.

I never heard from him.

One evening, about a week later, I sat at my kitchen table and called my cousin Arthur, a lawyer with a specialty in medical malpractice. With the article in my hands and Corey's blank gaze staring up at me, I filled Arthur in on what had transpired. I made sure to mention that he and his brothers were included in the family tree that was part of the publication. I asked if we had any legal recourse.

After taking some time to review the matter with his colleagues, Arthur told me that they believed our family should have been informed about the genetic bomb we carry. He explained what I already believed: Drs. Watters and/or Fitch should have contacted Audrey and my grandmother and told them what they had discovered—that the women in our family are carriers and have a fifty per cent chance of passing on the gene to any offspring.

In the spring of 2003, Andrew and I filed a lawsuit against the doctors for failing to inform us about our genetic health. Arthur told us that it would take years for our case to come to trial. He said Jacob would be close to eight years old by the time we got to court. He told us to prepare ourselves for a long and painful battle.

We listened to Arthur's words but we were determined. My family should have been given the information about our genetic structure. We should have had the facts needed to make informed decisions about whether we wanted to risk bringing children with an incurable disease into the world.

I cannot imagine my life without Jacob, but I should have been told. And I couldn't let the doctors get away with it.

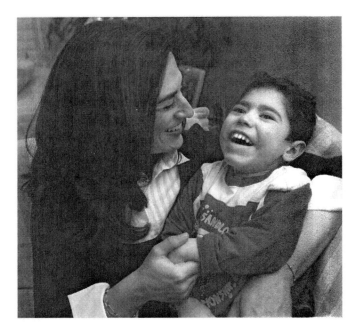

Marcy holding Jacob

— FEBRUARY 2007 —

*"Whether you think you can,
or think you can't — you're right."*

Henry Ford

CHAPTER 5

IT'S OFFICIAL—
WE HAVE A DIAGNOSIS

A few weeks after finding the article, Jacob and I found ourselves back at HSC, where he underwent a Visual Evoked Potential test to measure how efficiently he processed visual information. Jacob had electrodes placed all over his tiny head, wires transmitting his brain waves to a computer. As I held my terrified baby on my lap, carefully supporting his wobbly head, he screamed as images and lights were flashed on a screen that was inches from our faces.

Several weeks later I sat fidgeting on a hard chair in the sparsely furnished office that doubled as an examination room while I waited for the doctor to explain Jacob's visual acuity. As the pediatrician opened Jake's beige file, filled with three inches of medical reports, her eyes filled with tears and her voice lost the confident, professional tone that doctor's usually have. She gently explained that "the tests reveal that Jacob cannot see." I was stunned and did not know how to respond. I was being told that my curly haired son was blind. The test was wrong, but who would listen to me?

Jacob's various examination results were inconsistent with my experience. If he really was blind, why would he scream in fear every time a giraffe appeared on television during the Baby Einstein video? If he couldn't see, why would he start to squirm in fearful anticipation shortly before the scary giraffe portion of the movie? It was starting to become clear to me that the doctors didn't always have the answers. And sometimes, even when they think they did, they were wrong. I knew my son was able to see; he wasn't blind.

The doctors were doing their best, but I was the expert. During one of our many hospital visits, a doctor told me that he wanted to surgically remove a piece of Jacob's skin for analysis. I asked why. I wanted to know if the results would lead to a treatment or if it was simply to add more details to Jacob's already voluminous medical file. At another appointment, a specialist suggested a second MRI, which involved sedating my son. I weighed the potential benefits against the risks—of not being able to remove the breathing tube required for the anesthetic. Jacob's paralyzed vocal cords increase the risk that once intubated, he would not be able to be successfully extubated. As my confidence grew, so did my voice. I decided that any medical test or procedure that Jacob would undergo must have the potential benefit of bringing us closer to a treatment. I would not let him suffer for the sake of gathering more information that would be useful only in the context of academic publications about rare disorders.

When Jacob was eleven months old, I was at home playing with him when the telephone rang. Dr. Feigenbaum informed me that one of the many tests we'd agreed to had come back positive. He had Pelizaeus-Merzbacher disease (PMD) and my mother, my grandmother and I were confirmed carriers. I had never heard of this disease and didn't know what the diagnosis meant.

Initially, it was a relief to have a name to attach to his symptoms. But when I started asking questions, that relief turned to dismay. I was informed that there was no cure and no treatment was available. Further research revealed that my son's symptoms would worsen, his needs would become more complex, and his health would become more precarious. One website stated a lifespan of ten years and others predicted twenty. The National Institute of Health describes Pelizaeus-Merzbacher disease as a rare, progressive, degenerative central nervous system disorder in which coordination, motor abilities, and intellectual function deteriorate. The prognosis is poor, with progressive deterioration until death.

I was no longer sure that having a diagnosis was a good thing. Jacob wasn't going to get better. It wasn't fair, I kept thinking. According to our doctor, the only option was to treat each new symptom as it appeared. If his muscles start to tighten or spasm, we could try a muscle relaxant. If he develops seizures, we could give him anti-convulsant medication. If his spine starts to curve, he could undergo orthopedic surgery to fix the scoliosis. If his breathing worsens, doctors could surgically implant a tracheostomy tube. The list of how Jacob's body might deteriorate went on and on. I couldn't accept that this was our only choice. My role as a mother was to keep my son happy, healthy and safe. I would not sit back and wait for this disease to destroy my son.

• • •

Jacob's increasing number of doctor's appointments presented a unique challenge for us—aside from the basic necessities like Andrew having to book time off work or the ridiculous cost of hospital parking. My son's six-time a day feedings were still our biggest challenge and the situation would worsen when we were out of the house. Without fail, each time he was hooked up to the feeding tube and the pumped breast milk would begin to drip into his stomach, he would wail in pain. We were never able to figure out the reason for his yelling but it was awful. He would scream, choke and vomit. But we had to persist. We had been instructed by the doctors to keep feeding him, even though each drop must have felt like fire in his stomach. He needed the calories to get strong and grow.

Dealing with this routine around appointments was especially hard, particularly the ones at the hospital, because the doctors' schedules never ran on time and we were constantly waiting, sometimes for hours. I learned how to feed my son without an IV pole from which to hang his milk. I began to get creative, using coat hooks, filing cabinets or doors to suspend his bottles so gravity could help push the milk into his stomach through the tubes.

I dreaded medical appointments that occurred during or just after a feed. I would find myself having to sit motionless on an uncomfortable plastic chair—sometimes even a child-size chair, without armrests—and hold Jacob for the two hours he required to maximize his chances of keeping most of his feed in his stomach. More often than I care to remember, when the doctor finally entered the room and started the examination, which usually involved asking me a slew of questions, I was exhausted from the effort of holding Jake in an uncomfortable position, his sweaty head soaking through my sleeve. Or the doctor would sit in front of me, watching as I tried to clean Jacob's partially digested milk off my clothes or mop up a puddle of vomit that had landed on the floor.

We had so many meetings where I was covered in vomit, reeking from the odour. It's no wonder doctors were in a rush to end our sessions so quickly!

• • •

Around the same time we received the devastating PMD diagnosis, a wonderful, amazing thing happened: Jacob learned to smile. We captured one of his earliest grins in a photograph, an image of a little boy with pudgy cheeks and a big smile plastered across his toothless face. Each time I look at it, that photo transports me back to that magical moment. Jacob's smile, the one that took so many months to develop, was a turning point for me. I didn't realize it at the time, but in hindsight, that one moment allowed me to stop looking at Jacob with sadness.

Jacob's smile allowed me to uncover reserves of strength and courage located somewhere deep, deep inside me. I started to question the medical professionals. I began to realize they did not have all the answers, and even though many were reluctant to admit it, I learned they knew little about how to help Jacob. But as time passed, as I became more comfortable with the tiny fighter who is my son, I realized that I could not depend solely on the doctors for the answers. Jacob is *my* son. I know him so much better than a doctor who examines him for ten minutes, regardless of the plethora of degrees hanging on that doctor's office wall.

It was still excruciatingly painful to watch other children move effortlessly when my son could not. It still tore at my heart to listen to a toddler's childish babble when Jacob's only sound was crying. But my focus started to shift, slowly, to celebrate the joys that Jacob brought into my life. I began to appreciate the beauty of his smile and notice how his enormous green eyes would sparkle underneath the canopy of long black eyelashes when he heard someone sneeze. I praised each painstakingly slow movement of his hands as he tried to touch a toy placed on the tray in front of him. And, to my surprise, he tried even harder with each positive encouragement.

At one year old, and weighing just thirteen pounds, my son struggled each day of his life. It still wasn't fair, but if Jacob could find reasons to smile, so could I.

"Although the world is full of suffering,
it is full also of the overcoming of it."

Helen Keller

CHAPTER 6

A WHOLE NEW WORLD

Shortly after receiving the PMD diagnosis, I shifted my research from trying to figure out the cause of Jacob's rare symptoms to learning everything I could about the disorder that affected my baby.

Early on, years before Facebook and social media sites that link families like mine, I stumbled across a website for the PMD Foundation, an American organization devoted to helping families who are affected by PMD. I learned a lot about the genetics of the disease and noticed a phone number under the Contacts & Links tab. I took a deep breath and summoned the courage to dial. I was connected to Jeff, the father of a PMD boy a few years older than Jacob. It was the first conversation I had with someone who was living through the same medical challenges we were.

I finally found someone who had once been as lost as I still was and he offered some encouraging words. Jeff told me about his son, Jack, who had many of the same symptoms as Jacob, and explained how he was managing to cope with Jack's struggles. When my questions shifted from the personal to the medical, he suggested I contact Dr. Jim Garbern, a neurologist who specializes in PMD.

Jim and I traded emails and phone numbers. A few days later, on a Sunday afternoon in late spring, my phone rang. When I answered it, I was surprised to hear that it was Dr. Garbern on the other end of the line. Until then, not one of Jacob's many doctors had spoken to me on the phone. Dr. Garbern had never met Jacob and he was calling me on a Sunday. Immediately, I knew he was a special and caring physician.

As I sat down on the stairs that were just past our living room, Jim stated that he would be pleased to answer any questions I had. This was clearly a week for firsts, because this was also my first conversation with a medical professional who could actually provide some answers. Jim was an expert in PMD and he had examined more PMD children than anyone else in North America. I was excited to chat with him, but also nervous to ask the really hard questions. I didn't want to lose the hope I had that my baby would be okay.

We spent close to an hour on the phone. Jim patiently provided responses to my queries and solutions to some of the problems we were encountering with Jacob. He explained more about PMD than any physician we'd encountered since receiving our diagnosis. Jim generously took time out of his weekend to converse with me. I wanted to introduce him to some of Jacob's doctors and show them what they could learn from Jim's approach to patients. He is what every doctor should strive to be.

I didn't want the conversation to end! I wanted to squeeze every bit of information out of him and build my mental database of knowledge. I desperately wanted to understand everything about PMD: what I could expect, how it would progress, and what I needed to do to fix it. I wanted Jim to teach me what I could do to protect my small, helpless son from the ravages of this disease.

From the moment of Jacob's birth until I connected with Jeff, we had been alone. It was as if we were stranded on an island. Even once we received a diagnosis, there were very few assurances and little comfort given by our doctors. They simply didn't know what to do. They had never seen a patient with PMD since their only information was taken from a few paragraphs in a medical school text book. But once we connected with real PMD experts like Jeff, who had the hands-on, day-to-day experience of living with a PMD child, and Jim Garbern, who had personally met and examined hundreds of PMD boys, it was like a curtain was lifted. We could finally get a sense of what it truly meant to have PMD.

As wonderful as this was, the pictures these men painted were far from rosy. The prognosis was grim and the struggles were innumerable. But knowing we were not alone gave us some measure of comfort.

During our discussion, Jim told me about an upcoming conference on PMD. He explained that in a few months' time a group of researchers would be gathering in Delaware to review their PMD findings, and they were inviting PMD families to attend.

Andrew and I did not hesitate. We *had* to attend this meeting. As the date approached, I made arrangements for Jacob's care, ensuring that nurses would be with him twenty-four hours a day for the three days we would be away. He was too fragile to travel. My parents generously agreed to travel to Toronto and stay in our house with Jacob and the nurses.

The first two days of the meeting were held at the hotel where the families were staying. Walking through the lobby when we arrived, Andrew and I saw several children in wheelchairs. We huddled close together, whispering and wondering whether these kids had PMD. Neither of us had ever met another PMD child, so we didn't know what to expect. We checked into our room, nervous and anxious to begin learning from experts about the disease that was slated to destroy our son's body.

We met with Jim and several other physicians early the following morning. Jim requested that we bring Jacob's medical file so we could discuss his symptoms in detail. We were introduced to a researcher, Grace Hobson, who had performed the initial PMD testing on my family. One of the first things Grace told me was to ignore the information on the Internet that discusses the lifespan for PMD. She said that most kids with PMD, regardless of the severity of the disease (and Jacob's was among the most severe), live longer than the ten years stated on the websites I found. It sounds crazy, but that was good news. My son likely wouldn't die before he turned ten. The conference was off to a powerful start.

By mid-morning the session was formally underway and the first speaker approached the podium. I looked around the room and counted thirty attendees. I remember thinking that they didn't look like parents of disabled children, although I wasn't sure what that would look like. I sat transfixed, staring at the speaker, trying to take in all the information he was sharing. I was frantically taking notes, similar to the way I had in university, trying to capture the essence of each statement. Andrew, sitting in the seat to my left, simply listened. He didn't even have a pen or paper.

By lunchtime I was mentally tired. It was hard to concentrate so intently, having been out of school for so many years. The emotional aspect of the topic under discussion was also taking a toll. I was trying to soak up the information, but unlike my university days, it was not for a test. I wanted to absorb everything because I needed it to help my son. I believed that his future depended on it.

Andrew and I sat together over our meal and discussed what we'd heard. Despite our radically different learning styles, Andrew, the consummate software engineer, sucked up the clinical information and processed it. I understood the disease, how it was transmitted and how it eats away at the nervous system of its host. Andrew heard the same words as I did but understood them on a completely different level. By the end of the day, he was sitting at the doctors' table asking very detailed questions while a speaker was discussing physiotherapy exercises to try on PMD kids. A paper napkin served as their blackboard and one of the physicians started drawing sodium ion channels to properly answer my husband's questions. One response would lead to another, more sophisticated question. By the end of the second day, the doctors realized that Andrew's understanding of the molecular mechanism of PMD was catching up to theirs. He challenged them with his questions.

I knew my husband was smart, but I didn't realize how intelligent he was until that meeting. He even pointed out a typo on a presenter's slide when he noticed the speed of the neural transmission was off by a factor of ten. Like me, Andrew was on a mission to understand the disease that would ravage his son. I was deeply grateful to have him by my side as I struggled to make sense of the drawing on the paper napkin, despite my undergraduate degree in Anatomical Science.

Processing the information was hard but meeting the PMD kids was heartbreaking. There were boys of various ages, ranging from two to sixteen, in strollers and wheelchairs. One little boy, who had a milder form of the disease than Jacob, got around with the aid of a walker. None of the children spoke. Some had G-tubes, a couple had ventilators and all were painfully thin. It was one thing for me to understand the disease, but to see how it manifests itself was brutally and overwhelmingly painful. Everywhere I looked I saw another wheelchair. I couldn't help but envision how Jacob would look when he was the same age as these children, but at the same time, I couldn't really picture it.

At lunch on the second day, I sat next to Laura, the mother of ten-year-old Jared. Laura explained the therapy she does with her son on a daily basis. She spends a lot of time moving his legs and ensuring his muscles are stretched, as recommended by the physiotherapist they work with at home. But the bulk of her time is dedicated to feeding Jared. Unlike Jacob, Jared eats by his mouth, although it takes hours and hours to complete a meal. And despite the time devoted to spooning pureed food into her son's waiting mouth, he is still extremely underweight. What impressed me the most—and left a lasting image imprinted in my brain—was witnessing Jared communicate. Through his signal—a smile for yes— he told me that Laura was a good cook, better than his dad.

All the parents I spoke with during the conference confirmed something I already knew to be true: despite the test results and the conventional wisdom about the cognitive abilities of kids with PMD, their children all understood things, were able to learn and were constantly underestimated. I saw this myself, time and time again with Jacob.

• • •

Andrew and I boarded the plane home drained yet energized. We were exhausted from concentrating so hard, focusing on the detailed material and absorbing what it meant for our son. But we were confident that we had made good contacts within the PMD community. We'd met other families and established relationships with the key PMD researchers in the U.S. We'd confirmed what we had suspected: that there was no PMD research underway in Canada. We now had contact information for respected PMD experts to call when we had questions that Jacob's doctors were unable to answer.

And we were starting to understand the medical research and the direction in which the researchers were heading.

Naively, I tried to reassure myself that Jacob wouldn't look as broken as the children we saw because he'd had a G-tube since birth and had not damaged his lungs from multiple aspirations. He was receiving proper nutrition because we didn't need to spend hours trying to coax a few spoonfuls of cereal down his throat like some of the other parents did. And my son's limbs would stay loose and not spasm because we'd started physiotherapy when he was still an infant. Jacob had the benefit of early intervention while the children I met did not. These thoughts provided me with some comfort over the next few years.

I honestly believed that Jacob would be different. He would beat the disease and I wouldn't stop searching until we found a cure.

Andrew, Jacob and Marcy
— DECEMBER 2010 —

"Learn avidly.
Question repeatedly what you have learned.
Analyze it carefully.
Then put what you have learned
into practice intelligently."

Confucius

CHAPTER 7

RUN LITTLE MOUSE RUN

I actively searched for people who could help cure Jacob of this horrendous disease. Anytime someone mentioned a research project that might apply to PMD, I read it. If a friend suggested I call someone who knew something about myelin, I called. I tried to follow up on any potential lead I came across, still desperately trying to ease my son's symptoms.

A child's brain is pliable and new neural pathways are constantly developing. I knew that our best chance of curing Jacob would happen before he turned three. At that magical age, brain development slows and the degenerative aspects of PMD become more evident. Three was my deadline so I was working as hard as I could to make something happen before the proverbial window closed.

Through a cousin of a friend's husband's neighbor, I was led to a researcher who had been involved with a clinical trial of HP184, a drug that was initially developed for Alzheimer's patients. When the clinical results proved ineffective, the medication was shelved until someone thought to evaluate it's effectiveness for speeding up nerve transmission in spinal cord injury. Very early test results were impressive.

After a few telephone conversations, Andrew and I drove an hour to meet this scientist, who generously shared the data with us. We discussed the potential effectiveness of this compound for nerve fibers that were damaged from ineffective myelin formation, as is the case in children with PMD.

Concurrent with this discovery, I watched an old movie from 1990 titled *Lorenzo's Oil*. I remembered the movie, starring Nick Nolte and Susan Sarandon, from when it was released. It is a true story about a family's quest to find a cure for their son's degenerative disease. I didn't see it when it was in theatres because the topic did not appeal to me. I remember thinking that I didn't want to go to a movie to be depressed.

But watching *Lorenzo's Oil* from my current perspective, that of a mother searching for a cure for her child, was anything but depressing. If anything, it was uplifting and encouraging. It reinforced my determination and taught me about the strength it takes to battle the medical system. Inspired by the story, I contacted Augusto Odone, Lorenzo's father, through the website of his research foundation, The Myelin Project.

After several long conversations about Jacob over the course of a few weeks, Augusto invited Andrew and me to a Round Table he was organizing in Virginia in March 2004. He was gathering top PMD researchers from around the globe to brainstorm innovative treatments. I'm not sure if our discussions spurred him to plan this meeting or if it was something he was already considering. Regardless, it was a proactive way to help us find a cure so Andrew and I made arrangements to attend.

The conference was small and productive. There were twelve researchers from the U.S. and Europe and a few families, also from the U.S. and Europe. We were the only Canadian representatives. The tables were organized into a square, with doctors seated around the perimeter. The families were gathered at the foot of the square, like an audience watching a play. We sat and listened to the discussion, and heard ideas and theories being tossed around. The families were invited to listen but not encouraged to contribute to the conversation.

As we neared the end of the second day, I stood up and presented the data I'd collected on HP184. I explained its origins and shared the results of the nerve transmission study. Although the skeptics in the group tried to discount the data, a few researchers were intrigued.

Over dinner that night, Andrew and I had several conversations with researchers—including Jim Garbern—who were curious about HP184. A few doctors wanted to learn more about this compound and evaluate whether there was any possibility of using it to help treat PMD.

Upon our return home, I had another conversation with Jim Garbern about HP184. The initial results were so compelling that he contacted Sanofi-Aventis, the pharmaceutical company in question, to gain access to this compound.

Around the same time that we stumbled onto this drug, Andrew and I were searching for a way to raise money to fund research into PMD treatments. We knew that in order to gather large donations, we had to issue tax receipts. I started investigating the process of creating a charitable foundation so that we could establish ourselves as a "real" organization to collect money for research. Unfortunately, the process proved too slow and we were anxious to begin collecting funds right away, especially since the new drug seemed so promising. We were reluctant to spend the better part of a year on the steps needed to become registered as a charity.

Through mutual friends, Andrew and I were put in touch with Jeff and Ellen Schwartz, parents of a child with Canavan's disease, another myelin disorder. Jacob Schwartz is five years older than our Jacob, and the impetus behind Jacob's Ladder: The Canadian Foundation for Control of Neurodegenerative Disease. This is a charitable organization created by Jeff and Ellen to raise funds for neurodegenerative research.

After several meetings, Andrew and I formed an alliance with Jacob's Ladder to raise donations for funding PMD research. The monies raised by us for PMD research would be held in a separate account so that we could direct the funds to PMD-related projects as long as they were consistent with the overall research mandate of Jacob's Ladder.

While working on cementing this administrative relationship, Jim, Andrew and I set about designing a study to investigate the potential effectiveness of HP184 in treating PMD.

Navigating the world of medical research is agonizingly bureaucratic and frustratingly slow. It took an inordinate amount of time, close to two years, until we were given the go-ahead to conduct a small-scale study to evaluate the efficacy of the drug in mice with PMD.

Through generous donations from family and friends, Andrew and I raised enough money to fund this ground-breaking research. It was the first study that had the potential to treat PMD symptoms and we were hopeful that the results would be overwhelmingly positive. We dreamed that it was the miracle cure we were waiting for with Jacob nearing three years old; our time was running out.

For Jacob, daily life was still a tremendous challenge. In February 2005, he weighed twenty-three pounds and was on five medications, three of which were to control his frequent vomiting and retching. He was still fed every four hours around the clock and protested during many of his meals. He was, however, demonstrating some language comprehension and would sometimes nod his head "yes" in response to a question. It became evident to those around him that he was not blind since he was able to focus his gaze on toys that were placed in front of him. He was making progress, albeit at a slow pace, but he was growing and understanding people and things around him. Watching him smile in response to an image or story took my breath away. After waiting so long to see his first smile, it was something that to this day, I have never taken for granted.

His smiling, his sight—these were positives, but we wanted more. We wanted a cure. A producer from ABC's *Nightline* heard about our quest and wanted to film our developing story. The producer and a cameraman accompanied Andrew and me to Detroit in the spring of 2005 to capture the first injection of HP184 in a lab mouse on film. We were understandably nervous—we had so much hope riding on the little rodents. The camera zoomed in close to our faces and recorded the hope in our hearts and disappointment in our faces when the furry brown creatures with the long pink tails didn't show an improvement minutes after receiving the drug.

We left the lab deflated but rationalized that we hadn't really expected an instantaneous cure. We agreed that perhaps the mice needed to receive the drug for a longer period of time, as outlined in the research protocol. Maybe we would see a measurable improvement over time. We didn't need a complete cure—a gradual improvement or even a halt to the degeneration would also be positive.

After saying our goodbyes to Jim and his staff, I handed a photo of Jacob to one of the laboratory technicians. It was the picture of

Jacob's first smile. It was important for me to know that the lab techs were aware that a little person was the impetus behind the research. I wanted to ensure that they would see and remember the face of the young boy whose future was riding on the outcome of this study.

Three months later, the research was complete. A video was forwarded to Andrew, who agreed to show it to me for the first time when the *Nightline* crew was with us the following day. With another camera in my face and a microphone clipped to my sweater, I fixed my eyes on the screen as Andrew launched the video on his laptop. I watched the grainy footage and saw the mice hobbling along a table. There was a clear and definitive improvement in the gait and tail control of the mice post-HP184 treatment. It was working! The drug had helped the mice! To say we were ecstatic was an understatement. I kept staring at the images, replaying the video over and over. The results were better than we had expected. We had our miracle and my baby was going to be cured.

At least that's what I thought for a little while.

Despite what I saw on the video, the final analysis that came in a few weeks later stated that "the data did not show a statistically significant improvement" in the mice. In simple terms, it meant that the improvement was not observed in enough mice to make it worthwhile to continue funding additional experiments. I was crushed. It felt like the floor had fallen out from under me. I just couldn't believe it. The mice had clearly had a recovery that was caught on camera—everyone who watched the *Nightline* episode saw it too. I did not understand why the analysis was not supportive of this and was certain there must have been an error. Andrew and I pleaded with the group to redo the study, to no avail.

During the experiment, we were anxiously looking for a Canadian doctor to support our efforts. We wanted someone to objectively analyze the data with the hopes that if the results looked promising, he or she would advocate on our behalf to allow Jacob to receive the drug under medical supervision. Because the study was being conducted in the U.S., there would be a plethora of paperwork and approvals needed to obtain the drug for a Canadian patient—even if the results were outstanding. Despite our pleas, we were unable to find a physician willing to partner with us. The mediocre test results combined with a lack of a Canadian medical champion drove us into the proverbial brick wall.

We were out of options. Although we believed the medication to be effective, no doctors were willing to help. They told us that it was better to let the disease progress than to attempt to halt it and be faced with unknown side effects. They did not want to assume the risk associated with trying a new drug. We were told by several physicians that they were not willing to take responsibility for prescribing a drug that did not have years of data behind it. But we weren't asking for someone to blindly administer the drug. We wanted someone to help us evaluate whether the benefit outweighed the risks and then, if it seemed reasonable, to prescribe it. Nobody was interested.

We didn't get our miracle and Jacob's window was closing. At this point, we were out of research options.

"I have never let my schooling interfere with my education."

Mark Twain

CHAPTER 8

THE BUBBLE BURSTS

I only remember bits and pieces of the first years of Jacob's life. In my mind, the images are dark, probably to match my mood at the time. His early years were filled with tests and heartbreaking results. We were told that he would never walk, swallow or live to be a teenager. I would enter each doctor's office with a knot in my stomach, prepared for the inevitable crushing news about something my son would not be able to do.

Gradually, as Jacob and I grew stronger together, he physically and I mentally, we ventured out of the safety bubble of our house and into school, where he was finally exposed to other kids.

One of the clearest memories I have of that time was walking into Zareinu Educational Centre for the first time. Zareinu is a special school run by the Toronto Orthodox Jewish community for Jewish children with special needs. It's different from all the other programs in the city because it is primarily a therapy centre. Unlike the other programs I investigated, this school provides hands-on therapy, as much as each child requires. Under one roof, Jacob could receive physiotherapy, occupational therapy, speech therapy and music therapy. The physio and occupational therapists who were currently treating him were employed there. Our decision to attend Zareinu had very little to do with its faith-based aspect. It was simply the place where "the best therapists in the city worked," according to the many doctors we consulted.

I went to the school to check out the Infant Intervention Program to see whether it would be appropriate for Jacob. On paper, the place was great. However, as with all big decisions, this one wasn't a slam dunk. We had to weigh the pluses and minuses. On the plus side, Jacob would receive all the therapy he required in one place. I wouldn't have to plan as many individual appointments around his feeding schedule and our frequent doctors' appointments. He would receive speech therapy, which he had not started yet, and he would be introduced to music therapy, provided by the president of the Canadian Association for Music Therapy. But he would be in a classroom with other children who carried an assortment of germs. I wondered whether bringing him to the program would expose him to viruses that could overwhelm his weak immune system. It was not an easy decision.

My first visit to Zareinu stands out, in my mind, as one of the most difficult things I have ever done. Armed with clear directions, I entered the complex and drove down the steep driveway into the underground parking lot that the school shared with a synagogue and elementary school. After being buzzed through the security doors, I walked up the handful of stairs to the school. Although there was a small lift next to the stairs, it was locked and I later learned that very few people in the building had access to the key.

I continued down the dimly lit hallway to the office, barely noticing the old beige paint littered with black scuff marks. All I could see were the wheelchairs and funny looking equipment littering the hallways. The silence that surrounded me was deafening. Unlike most elementary schools, which are constantly humming with the sounds of rambunctious children, this school was quiet.

I was escorted to the Infant Program and invited to watch for the morning to see how the program was structured. The staff could not have been warmer or more welcoming. I sat in the back of the room, observing the eight children and their mothers. Each child was engaged in an activity, occasionally working one on one with a therapist. There were a lot of toys placed at various stations around the room, all chosen with a therapy goal in mind: to stimulate vision, to introduce various textures, to reinforce cause and effect, to challenge fine motor skills and more.

I studied the children. Two obviously had Down syndrome since their characteristics were easy to identify. But there were a couple of children who could sit without support and didn't have any obvious disability. I wondered why they were in the program.

My breath caught in my throat when I realized that if Jacob were to attend the program, he would be the child with the most challenges in the group. I began to realize that if these children, who to my untrained eye looked healthy, needed the intensive therapy the program offered, Jacob most certainly did. It was in this brightly coloured, child-friendly room that I started to come to terms with the fact that my son was severely impaired. This was a handful of his peers and all were clearly more advanced than he was. It was a very painful realization and I had to fight back my tears as I sat on the kid-sized blue plastic chair.

When I walked back into the hallway an hour later, I remember wanting to leave the building and run to my car. I remember wishing that I would never have to come back. But I also remember realizing that Jacob *needed* to come and benefit from what they were offering.

• • •

It took me a few months, but by the start of the following school year, in September 2003, I had enrolled Jacob at Zareinu. He was sixteen months old and a mere thirteen pounds. His health was still frail and he choked several times a day.

Until then, the only time Jacob left the house was to go to appointments for doctors and therapy. I was determined to give Jacob the best, so he and I went to Barb's house twice a week for occupational therapy and to Ester's house three times a week for physiotherapy. He hated the physio appointments and protested the entire time. In the beginning, a few family members would occasionally accompany us to physio; they were curious and wanted to see what exercises Jacob did. But the sound of his incessant crying and his eventual choking were too much for them to bear and I ultimately brought him to therapy by myself. For me, knowing that Ester and Barb worked at Zareinu was a big plus (two, actually!) for having Jacob enrolled in the program. We reduced our visits to Ester to once or twice a week and to once a week for Barb.

Had Jacob been given a choice, he would have stated that Ester's involvement at Zareinu was reason enough to *not* enroll in the program! Looking back on it now, it seems like we were subjecting Jacob to torture, but I wanted to make sure we did everything possible to strengthen his muscles and prevent the deterioration that is a clinical feature of PMD. I believed I was doing the best thing for my son.

Because Jacob has a weak immune system, Andrew and I were worried that his exposure to other kids would be very dangerous for him. At this stage of his life, a simple cold was life-threatening. Ellen, Zareinu's Early Intervention Specialist, understood this and set aside toys exclusively for Jacob's use. Each morning when we arrived, a large baggie with his name on it, filled with toys chosen specifically for Jacob, was placed in a corner of the room. The toys were brightly coloured, different textures and some made sounds. All had been selected to stimulate his various senses. This corner became Jake's area. We even brought our own chair so we wouldn't need to worry about whose germs Jacob would sit on. The staff was sympathetic to my son's health issues and accommodated his needs without hesitation. If they thought we were being neurotic, they didn't let on.

We spent that year, two mornings a week, at school. I was late most days and would arrive carrying a drenched little boy. Invariably, on the drive to the school Jacob would choke and I would be forced to stop my car in the middle of the road to attend to my son. I would flick my hazard lights on and turn around in the front seat to try and help Jacob. More often than not, the episode would end with a projectile vomit that necessitated a complete clothing change as soon as we entered the classroom.

Jacob received a lot of one-on-one therapy from the instructors in the program, including Ester and Barb, and he also participated in music circles with the other seven children in the group. Wanda introduced Jacob to a variety of musical instruments, including cymbals, shakers and his favourite, the guitar. She sang for Jacob, and waited patiently for him to lift his small fisted hand for his turn to strum the strings on her instrument. As soon as the first note was out of her mouth, Jacob would smile.

The professionals in the group were wonderful with Jacob. Their demeanor was welcoming and always encouraging. For the first time since his birth, I had a place to go to interact with other mothers of children with challenges. It was a friendly atmosphere, warm and accepting.

Jake enjoyed the classroom activities, including speech and occupational therapy, but he still detested physiotherapy. Everyone at the school quickly became familiar with the piercing wails that emanated from the physio room when it was Jake's turn on the black padded table. His protests started as I carried him down the hall, peaking as we crossed the threshold into the treatment room. Ester has a reputation of being tough with kids, working through their screams and ignoring their complaints, so the achievements made under her guidance were remarkable. We've met several parents who are convinced their children are walking because of her. I was hoping Jacob would have similar phenomenal results.

In September 2004, after one year in the program, Jacob graduated to the Nursery room, which he attended five mornings a week without me by his side. His teachers joked that he should have a pager because he spent so much time out of the class, either having one-on-one therapy or zooming around the halls learning how to maneuver a power wheelchair and walker. The skills he was working on were constantly reinforced in his classroom. He received intensive therapy and loved the program.

One day, when I came to pick up Jake, two staff members excitedly explained that he seemed to love listening to Andrea Bocelli music. When my response didn't match their enthusiasm, they explained what had transpired during their class outing to a nearby mall. While they were waiting in a store, Andrea Bocelli's "Amore" was playing on the speakers. It immediately became clear to Norma, Jake's favourite assistant, that he liked the music. When the singer's voice rose in tune with the music, Jacob began to vocalize and move his arms. When the music slowed down, so did Jacob's intonations. Surprised and encouraged by the description, I was eager to see if it would happen again. On our way home, we stopped at a store and I purchased the CD.

Later that afternoon, I popped the disk into the CD player and waited. As the music increased in intensity during the first song, "Amapola," Jacob repeated the behaviour Norma had enthusiastically recounted. Shocked, I began to laugh and encouraged Jacob to continue his singing. And he did! Over and over again, even moving his arms to emphasize the size of the sounds. It was incredible! I called my mother on the phone and held the receiver to her ear so she could hear her grandson sing opera. Simply describing his singing wasn't good enough; I needed her to hear it for herself.

Jacob was thriving—he loved the staff in his class, and they adored him. And he was never left on his own; there was always a willing assistant to help him complete a task or to talk to him. But all of this attention had a serious drawback—Jacob was unable to find a way to entertain himself if left alone for a few moments. His limited movement made handling toys or books challenging and because he was non-verbal, he could not voice his needs.

Andrew and I quickly realized that if Jacob were ever to become a big brother, he would need to learn how to spend some time amusing himself.

$$\bullet \quad \bullet \quad \bullet$$

The decision to have more children after Jacob was diagnosed with PMD was colossal. Was it selfish of us to bring a healthy child into a family with a child who required constant care?

When Andrew and I started exploring the idea of a sibling for Jacob, we thought it would be terrific for us. It would allow us to re-enter the "normal" world and experience the joys of parenthood as a "typical" parent, a mother who was fortunate enough to teach her child how to count to ten or hold a crayon and a father who could teach his child to ride a bicycle. Our parenting experience consisted mostly of medication administration, physical therapy and frequent doctors' appointments. It was easy to see that a healthy child would bring some much wanted normalcy into our lives. And now that we knew I was a carrier for PMD, it would be possible to test the fetus before birth to see if it had the defective gene.

But late at night, when Jacob was in the care of the nurse, we wrestled with the answers to a number of questions: What impact would having a disabled older brother have on a younger sibling? Would a sibling detract from the attention Jacob needed?

We reasoned that Jacob would have the opportunity to interact with another child, something he rarely did but seemed to enjoy. The stories we heard led us to believe that Jacob's hypothetical sister or brother would not be negatively affected by growing up in our family. In fact, with proper guidance, he or she would have a tremendous opportunity to thrive and become a special person because of our family's experiences.

When Jake was two-and-a-half years old, he became a big brother to healthy twin sisters. Tests conducted before they were born and repeated immediately following their births confirmed that they did not have the faulty gene that causes PMD. Unlike their mother, maternal grandmother and great-grandmother, Sierra and Jamie are not PMD carriers.

As infants, they were a handful, but it was so much easier parenting these two girls than it had been caring for their brother at the same age. I knew that if the girls were hungry, they would eat, if they were tired, they would sleep and if they cried, they were not at risk of choking. They never needed me to thread a suction tube down their throat to clear their airways. Sierra and Jamie's arrival altered our family dynamics and added a whole new level of excitement to our home. They were such a welcome addition.

As I watched my girls explore their surroundings, a mix of emotions ran through me. I oscillated between awe at the ease with which Sierra and Jamie knew how to shake a rattle or turn the page in a book and a soul-numbing sorrow knowing that Jacob was unable to hold his beloved guitar by himself.

The increased activity in our house pleased Jacob. He smiled when we placed him on the sofa with a sister on either side of him. His eyes sparkled when he was positioned in the front of the double stroller, listening to his little sisters babble as they squished in the seat behind him.

The girls were early talkers and very curious. As Sierra was nearing her third birthday, she asked me why Jacob could not walk. Her innocent and appropriate question scared me. I knew that at some point they would notice that Jacob was different from their friends' older brothers. It was important to me that the girls were comfortable asking questions about their brother and I was determined to give them honest and age-appropriate answers that would help them understand Jacob but not scare them. Although she was satisfied with my response—that his legs don't work the same way hers do—I knew that this question would soon be followed by other more challenging ones.

When Sierra and Jamie blew out the candles on their Dora the Explorer birthday cake on their third birthday, Sierra pushed her hair away from her face and asked if I could put some cake in Jacob's feeding tube. She knew that her brother did not eat the same way she did, but she wanted him to enjoy something that she loved. As my eyes filled with tears, I told her that I was very proud of her attempt to share her cake with her brother.

THE BOY WHO CAN

Our family is not typical. Jacob still requires constant care, but making him an older brother was the right decision for us. Jake's younger sisters are happy, smart and curious girls. And they have a special brother with a contagious laugh that can be heard anytime they try to tickle him.

· · ·

Jacob progressed through the Nursery program and eventually moved into other classes.

He was showered with so much love and attention at Zareinu. When I entered the school to pick him up, I would often see a group of adults gathered around my little boy, each taking turns talking to him or playing with him. The attempt to teach him to play independently did not succeed—well meaning but enamored staff couldn't stay away from him. And he had a smile on his face that stretched as far as his little lips could go. He was in his element and I felt like he was in the right place.

Until he wasn't.

When a teacher administered a "standard assessment" suitable for toddlers to Jacob, who was then six, he became annoyed that she was ignoring his true abilities. He purposely gave false answers, as if to say "of course I know that the object in your hand is a pencil but since you insist on asking me such a ridiculous question, I will tell you that it is a truck." He laughed after each incorrect response.

A few teachers recognized Jacob's love of learning and worked diligently with him. I was told that my son was the smartest in the class and should be moved to a classroom that was focused on academic material and not the preschool format of play-based learning. While I campaigned to have Jacob moved into a classroom with

113

children who were as cognitively aware as he was, I was reminded of my earlier battle convincing skeptics that Jacob was not blind.

Despite my earlier experience—combined with day-to-day occurrences of Jacob being underestimated—I innocently believed this would be an easy task. I had the support of two teachers who ignored the assessment and were willing to confirm Jake's true abilities, and we identified an appropriate classroom. It seemed like an easy move. Boy, was I wrong.

After weeks of stalling on the part of the school principal, I was finally told that Jacob could "spend time" in the identified classroom. My joy quickly turned to shock when I learned that Jacob's time in the room would be limited to a couple of hours a week. I was frustrated by the administrator's refusal to look past Jacob's physical limitations and his insistence that Jake stay in an environment that was not challenging his academic abilities.

After a few months, I realized that my request to permanently move Jake into the more advanced classroom was being ignored. Despite conversations with the principal, who did not challenge the teachers' assessments of Jake's aptitude, I was unable to convince him to permit Jacob to spend more time in the other classroom. I was not given an explanation for the unwillingness to nurture Jacob's potential and I made the difficult decision to move my son to a new school. This move would mean that he would not have the daily physio, occupational and speech therapy sessions that, in the opinion of the "experts," were vital to his ongoing physical development. However, it would give him the opportunity to challenge his brain, something that he desperately enjoyed and deserved.

In February 2009, partway through the school year, Jacob left the only school he had ever attended and transferred to Sunny

View Public School, a part of the Toronto public school board and a school that catered to children with physical and other disabilities. Initially, he remained at Zareinu two mornings a week so that he could continue with the therapy and he spent the balance of the week at the new school.

He was assigned to a classroom with kids who didn't speak and didn't move independently, so that interacting with other kids, one of his favourite activities, was impossible. At first, the teacher didn't realize how much he understood and treated him like he didn't know anything. And because he couldn't speak, all he could do was cry and scream. He was trapped. Nobody was listening to him, and he had no clue why these things were happening until I explained. About a month later, I told him that the school had finally realized they put him in the wrong class and had promised to move him. I also told him he had to wait until the start of the next school year, even though there were still several months until the summer break.

By the start of the following school year, Jacob was enrolled full-time at Sunny View and no longer had the same amount of hands-on therapy. He had "consultations" with a physiotherapist on issues related to his wheelchair, stander and walker, and "consultations" with a speech therapist who provided suggestions to the classroom teachers on ways to help Jacob communicate. The only one-on-one therapy that Jacob received was his weekly occupational therapy session with Barb, whom he continued to see until her untimely death in 2010.

But the intense therapy trade-off was worth it. Jacob was given the chance to really learn! For the first time in his life, he was following parts of the Ontario curriculum.

As I listened to Cheryl Libman, Jacob's teacher, from across the table in the conference room in late September 2009, I knew I had made the right choice. A cozy feeling of warmth spread through my body when I heard her state that Jacob recognized the letters of the alphabet and the numbers one to ten, and could identify colours. My heart swelled with pride as Cheryl reported her observation to the group of five communication specialists gathered to discuss Jacob's communication abilities and needs. Finally, he was being taught at a level on par with his abilities. And there were kids in his class who ran and talked and played with him. People were always coming into the class because they heard his laugh halfway down the hall. His gigantic grin in the classroom was evidence he was enjoying the challenge.

Until he wasn't.

Fast-forward a school year: new teachers, new children and new routines. Cheryl left the school to take a job at Elkhorn Public School, another school within the Toronto public school system, and Jacob needed a new class. He was placed with great kids, some of whom were verbal and mobile, and who enjoyed interacting with my son. The teacher situation wasn't ideal—there were two instructors who job-shared and both worked part time. For one of the teachers, this was her first job; she had just received her teaching degree a few months earlier. And neither teacher knew my son.

One of the school's "selling" points is that they do their best to keep kids and teachers together for several years because it often takes a while for teachers to get to know the kids and learn the best ways to teach them. This was Jacob's third year at Sunny View and his third class placement.

I like to be aware of what my son is learning at school, so I can talk to him about it when he gets home and ask him "yes/no" questions about the material he might have covered, or if he enjoyed it. Vanessa taught on Mondays, Tuesdays and alternate Wednesdays, and Keri was there on Thursdays, Fridays and every other Wednesday. There was a lack of consistency if, for example, I wrote a question in Jake's communication book on Tuesday night and it was Keri's week to work on Wednesday. This was not the fault of the teachers; they were working their allotted hours and sticking to their schedules.

But I didn't have a sense of how Jacob's school day unfolded. When I kissed him goodbye in the morning and watched the bus driver secure his chair to all the hooks Transport Canada requires, I caught myself holding my breath. I knew where my son was going and when he would come home. But I was filled with a sense of helplessness bordering on dread because I had no way of knowing exactly what he would do during the day. All I learned about Jacob upon his return home is what was contained in the few short sentences his teacher wrote in his communication book: Jacob had art today; he laughed when Colin burped; he seemed tired. But there was no mention of having a shorter swim because there was nobody to change him, having his feed set up late because the nurse was busy with another student, or how he felt when he correctly identified his name from a series of words. Jacob can't tell me those things, nor can he confirm whether he was, in fact, tired or simply bored with the activities in the classroom. And he cannot share what he was thinking about when he was at school.

Jacob's school caters to children with special needs; all the students have some degree of physical impairment. Some are verbal and can express themselves, while others cannot speak and their ability to understand even the most basic words is questionable. And there are a lot of youngsters, like Jacob, whose communication and comprehension abilities fall somewhere in between the two extremes. Because the educators are so involved with these kids on a daily basis—teaching them, tending to their multitude of needs and trying, sometimes in vain, to control the aberrant behaviours— I think they sometimes forget that these children can't go home and discuss their day with family. As a parent, I crave this information. I hunger for it to get a sense of my son and his activities. I need it to monitor his day and make sure he is meeting the goals that were set for him at the beginning of the school year.

When my daughters come home from school, they talk about their day. Sierra is more effusive with her information but Jamie recounts some tidbits as well. If something major happens, if someone is mean to one of them or if one was the day's Special Helper, I'm sure to hear about it even before their seatbelts are fastened for the drive home. I am confident in the knowledge that if something were wrong, they would tell me about it and together we could try to remedy the issue.

But because Jacob can't speak, he can't tell me what happened during the day. I am at the mercy of what is written in the communication book—the few sentences that are meant to summarize his day.

When I started looking into the curriculum Jacob was receiving, I noticed that it was not aligned with the material other children his age were being taught in mainstream schools. Jacob was following an "alternate curriculum," one that had not been explained to me when I agreed to his placement at Sunny View. Upon further investigation, I learned that Jacob's teachers had the authority to modify his curriculum as they deem necessary. And because there were no other children of Jacob's age and cognitive ability in the school, he was placed with kids of varying ages. It took me over a year to realize that this meant that Jacob was not receiving his age-appropriate curriculum, modified or regular. In fact, because he changed classes, teachers, classmates and therapists each year, his educational foundation resembled Swiss cheese. One year he was taught at a grade-one level and the following year it was grade five.

This wasn't what I'd wanted. I'd wanted Jacob in our local school (impossible, I was told). It wasn't wheelchair accessible. I'd wanted him to be around "regular" kids, but Sunny View was a "special" school. Not for the first time in Jacob's life, things were not working out the way I'd hoped.

I broached this topic at Jacob's Identification, Planning and Review Committee (IPRC) meeting during the spring of 2011, when everyone involved in his care met to review his school year and start planning for the upcoming one. I requested that Jacob be placed in a regular classroom at a regular school for a scheduled block of time on a recurring basis. Although everyone at the meeting acknowledged the benefits of reverse integration, they were unsure about how to make it happen. There was concern about resources: his school did not have additional assistants to accompany Jacob, nor did they have a driver who could facilitate the transfer. And, most importantly, they didn't know of another school that would welcome such an unorthodox arrangement.

I wanted this for him because over the years Jacob had a variety of experiences with typically developing children and they were all positive. He has enjoyed listening to their little voices and being included in their games. And I love that the kids—often more so than the adults around them—have seen beyond Jacob's wheels and limited movement.

A couple of weeks after the IPRC meeting, I followed up with Jacob's principal and attempted to address the concerns that had been raised. I acknowledged the challenges in my request but felt that with some creative thinking, it might be possible. I said I would drive him to the school and would stay and help him during the placement. The arrangement I envisioned would not cost the school a penny. We both agreed to explore our contacts and see if we could find a placement.

We didn't have to look far and quickly located two schools that wanted to welcome my son. The school we chose, Elkhorn Public School, was the one where the teacher knew Jacob from a previous year. How wonderful it would be for Jacob and Cheryl to be together again, I thought. They made a great pair: energetic, motivating and loving teacher, and eager, attentive and adoring pupil.

Two days before Jacob's first day at Elkhorn, I met with Paul, the principal. As I sat in Paul's office and answered his questions about my son, I couldn't help but remember my not-so-fruitful conversation with another school administrator the last time I'd tried to have Jacob exposed to a similar type of student body, when he was five years old.

"It would be too traumatic for kids to be around your son" were the words she'd uttered when I inquired about having some of her students attend my son's school. At the time, her statement made me cringe with fury.

I questioned whether she meant the experience would be too traumatic for the students or for the teachers. She reiterated that according to her advisers, it would be "too traumatic for the students."

Although I knew she was wrong, a seed of doubt was planted in me. I was afraid that other people in similar positions would be equally small-minded, and I was worried about exposing my little boy to that destructive thinking. As I recalled that disturbing conversation from my seat in Paul's office, I physically shook my head in an effort to rid myself of those thoughts. Instead, I continued telling Paul about my son. He seemed genuinely interested and was impressed that Jacob had met Andrea Boccelli and was a pseudo-television star. I showed him the video on our website and recounted how the producer at ABC's *Nightline,* upon hearing about Jacob's love of Andrea Boccelli's music and my vain attempts to contact the superstar, arranged for us to attend Andrea's rehearsal prior to a concert he was performing in Niagara Falls. Jacob, Andrew, my brother, Norma (Jake's favourite assistant from Zareinu who was the first to notice Jacob's affinity for opera) and I drove to the private rehearsal and met the famous singer. It was clear to Paul that Jacob could add a lot of positive energy to his student body.

Later that day, when I explained to Jacob that Cheryl would be his teacher once a week, his mouth opened and he let out an excited scream, accompanied by some squirming in his chair. It was obvious this idea pleased him. But two days later as we drove to the school, Jacob started protesting and making noises. When I asked if he was scared and nervous, he nodded his head. I reassured him, saying I would stay with him as long as he wanted.

As I transferred Jacob from the van to his wheelchair, Cheryl came running over to us and began enthusiastically describing the plan for the afternoon. I couldn't help but smile when I saw the excitement on my son's face and heard the animation in Cheryl's voice. I asked Jacob if I could leave and he didn't hesitate before nodding his head affirmatively. I desperately wanted this event to be a success.

A few hours later, I walked into the school to pick up my son, anxious to learn how it had gone. I knew Jacob would be comfortable and safe with Cheryl but I wondered how the other kids would react to him. The description I received from Cheryl was only surpassed by the sights I witnessed the following week upon our return.

Students and teachers lined up to meet the newcomer. There were some questions, including "why is he wearing a wheelchair?" but these inquiries were posed with innocence and acceptance; there was no fear or trauma involved.

When I dropped him off the next time, Jacob was presented with a hand-drawn sign that read "Welcome Back, Jacob." The artists were three students who had not been able to meet him the previous week but wanted to be among the first to do so upon his return. It warmed my heart to witness the little people congregated around Jacob's wheelchair, bending down so he could see their faces as they introduced themselves. When it became apparent that Jacob thought sneezing was hysterical, the room filled with faux sneezes in attempts to elicit Jacob's contagious, full-body laughter. The scene filled me with a sense of contentment.

At the start of the next school year, in September 2011, Jacob was nine years old, entering grade four at Sunny View and, once again, in a new class with all new kids. This time he was the youngest in the class by several years. The other children were in grade six and one boy was in grade eight and graduating at the end of the year. I was told that the reason Jake was placed in this class was because there were no other kids of his age and cognitive ability at Sunny View. I couldn't help but think that he didn't really belong there. The teacher was very nice and liked to play guitar for him, but each day my son sat in a circle and counted how many days he had been at school. Reaching 100 was the goal but he had been doing this for the past three years—didn't they know he could count? I was at school frequently to meet with the teacher and review the curriculum to ensure that it was sufficiently challenging.

Jacob continued to attend Elkhorn on Friday afternoons in Cheryl's class. It was a great arrangement as it allowed him to participate in a new initiative at Sunny View. The Infinity Lab was a joint project between Sunny View and Tom Chau's group at Holland Bloorview, the same team that created Jake's adapted iPod. Jake was one of ten children chosen to take part in intensive communication training within the school.

A few times a week Jacob went to the Infinity Lab where Kat, Tania and Leslie helped him use his iPod. Jake excelled at this, a fact that gives me hope that one day Jacob will be able to tell people how he feels when he is underestimated.

Jacob received academic and social stimulation at Elkhorn and comprehensive iPod lessons and practice sessions at Sunny View. He was happy because he loved going to Elkhorn, the place where he belonged. He made real friends, for the first time in his life, and he was part of the class. He learned French, art and some social studies too. He even had play dates! Jake's friends came over to our house and he went to theirs. One of them even met Jake at his swimming lesson so they could swim together. It was so incredible to watch my son play with his friend in the water. And he was invited to two birthday parties—that's two more than ever before! Finally people understood him and treated him like the person he is.

I was so pleased with this arrangement and eager to let others know about Jacob's fantastic experience, so I wrote an article that was published in a local newspaper in early March 2012 to praise the Elkhorn administrators for allowing us to create this unconventional program for my son.

I was completely blindsided when, a few days after the article's publication, I was summoned to the principal's office at Elkhorn. As a result of the story, Paul had received two phone calls, one from the superintendent of the school district and another from the superintendent principal, Special Education, demanding that Jacob stop attending Elkhorn immediately. The reason: the school board administrators were terrified about the precedent this out-of-the-box arrangement would set. They were afraid that the families of other kids with special needs would overwhelm their office with similar requests. Nobody disputed that everyone involved benefited from Jacob's attendance at Elkhorn. But what was best for Jacob did not factor into the decision to banish my son from the school.

During Jake's life, I have been thrown some unexpected curve balls, but this one caught me completely off guard. I'd published the chronicle because I wanted to recognize the outstanding staff and students for treating my son like a person with feelings, something that doesn't occur as regularly as it should. Sitting in Paul's office, trying to hold back my tears (and then realizing it was a battle I had little chance of winning), I was stunned and furious. I asked Paul what our options were. (Even at the time I knew it was a good thing that the board didn't know I'd recently met with Howard Goodman, my local school trustee, to help advocate for Jacob to attend Elkhorn three full days a week the following year, instead of just part of one day!) Paul agreed to allow Jacob to come for a few more weeks, until Easter, thereby giving me some time to figure out my next step. But there was no way I was going to retreat quietly. Not a chance—this was too important.

A new battle was beginning. I was angry and determined to make things work with Elkhorn. I did my research. During the fall of 2011, I investigated three schools that might be a good fit for Jake. I wanted to find a school that would be as successful for him as Elkhorn was, and I thought that if he attended a school closer to home or one with more kids in wheelchairs who were following an academic curriculum, then maybe I wouldn't have to design a unique plan for Jake. But those schools were poor fits for reasons that included a lack of wheelchair accessibility and high student-to-teacher ratios. My research was conducted over the course of a few months and the plan to split the week between Sunny View and Elkhorn—the plan I had discussed with the trustee—was borne out of the information I collected. It wasn't simply designed to create trouble and cause my name to be synonymous with headaches. Why couldn't people comprehend that my son deserved to learn in an environment that challenged him and a social milieu where he could develop sustaining friendships? Full-time enrollment at Sunny View was not fulfilling that need.

The trustee and I met once in February but corresponded frequently by phone and email. Initially, our conversations were centred on Jacob attending two schools the following year, but when the article caused chaos to erupt, he stepped in to help. It didn't take long for the school board to back down and agree to allow Jake, who was viewed by his Elkhorn classmates as a member of their group, to finish off the school year the same way he had started it. But the bigger battle was just gaining momentum.

Howard cautioned me to be patient. He reassured me that he was doing everything in his power to make sure the Toronto District School Board (TDSB) senior officials, who were organizing a city-wide conference on inclusion in the public schools, realized how their refusal to welcome Jacob back to Elkhorn was contrary to everything they had been campaigning about with respect to children with special needs and the benefits of integrating these kids into the mainstream programs. It was ludicrous and hypocritical.

One Friday in late March 2012, when I was picking Jake up at Sunny View for his afternoon at Elkhorn, a tall blonde woman approached us and introduced herself as the superintendent, one of the women who was demanding that Jake stop attending Elkorn. She stated that she had found a new arrangement for "integration" for Jacob and wanted to meet with me to discuss it. Skeptical but always willing to listen, I arranged to meet with her in a few weeks' time.

As we sat around the small table in the Sunny View principal's office, the superintendent proceeded to extol the benefits of the new integration program she was creating for Jacob. She explained that he would be able to attend the school across the street as often as I wanted him to and would not be limited to an afternoon a week. She energetically explained how this arrangement would be expanded to include Jacob's classmates so he wouldn't be the lone participant. I was baffled; a year earlier when I had inquired about my son attending that very school, I was told that it was impossible because it was not wheelchair accessible. When I mentioned that fact, the superintendent barely paused long enough for a breath before telling me that he would be in the basement because that was the only level that would accommodate a wheelchair. When I asked what my son would be doing in the basement of the school, she explained: "He could watch the other kids participate in phys. ed."

My eyes popped open when I realized she was serious. I waited for the principal of Sunny View, whose office we were in, to speak up and advocate on Jacob's behalf and explain how inappropriate that solution was. Her support didn't come and I realized that I was once again on my own. This principal was not going to stand up for Jacob, and both women failed to realize how offensive and discriminatory the "proposal" was.

I had nothing further to discuss with these women who failed to see that Jacob sitting by the sidelines and watching able-bodied kids run and play ball is not the same as him learning alongside kids who embrace his differences and ask their parents to plan play dates with him after school. I knew it was pointless to try to convince them. It was evident that they lacked empathy for and understanding about kids like Jacob.

Over the course of the next three months, I encountered several more ignorant and inflexible senior TDSB staff doing their best to prevent Jacob from attending the only school that he truly belonged in. There were some who adamantly opposed Jacob's attendance at Elkhorn for reasons that had nothing to do with his ability. I was given excuses such as "how would the other parents at Elkhorn react to Jacob at the school?" and "if it's done for Jacob, we would have to do it for everyone" and, my favourite, "a parent is not allowed to choose a child's school placement."

The first time I'd proposed that Jacob attend Elkhorn three full days a week instead of the half-day a week he'd been attending since

May 2011, I was told that I was looking at an uphill struggle. I nodded my head, and I said I knew that, but I didn't know. Not really.

There was no way I would have predicted that what I thought was a reasonable request would cause such turmoil and upheaval at the head office of the TDSB. If someone had told me that the issue of my son's education would disrupt the lives of several senior administrators and bring some of the more progressive and empathic thinkers to tears on more than one occasion, I would have suggested they were exaggerating. And if I had been told that my son's schooling would be the subject of several television, radio and newspaper stories, I would have chuckled in disbelief.

It was never my intention to be a trailblazer. I was—I am—simply a mother advocating on behalf of her son because he cannot do it on his own. Jacob's PMD makes everything harder for him but it does not negate the fact that he deserves to be treated as a respected member of society. The treatment I received as his proxy was appalling and discriminatory. The excuses I was given for the delay in granting my request were insulting and offensive.

At the end of every phone conversation I had with a school board official during the spring and summer of 2012, I'd hang up the phone with trembling hands, my insides raging and my head feeling like it was going to explode. I couldn't understand how these people were able to ignore the fact that my son thrived during the year in which he'd been permitted to spend one afternoon a week at the school under discussion. He made friends. He learned alongside these kids, participating in his own way, even answering questions in French class.

As time passed and the fight escalated, my body had trouble adjusting to its new normal—a constant level of anxiety so high that breathing became a task I had to consciously remember to do. Nights became unbearable. I would wake with a start, gasping for air, terrified that I'd lost one of my kids somewhere, only to remember that the true source of my angst was Jacob's school situation.

I had many long and difficult months to ruminate over my request. I repeatedly asked myself if it was worth pursuing or whether I should give up the struggle. But each time, I came back to the same steadfast conclusion: this was the best thing for my son.

A father wrote a letter to the school board requesting them to allow Jacob to attend Elkhorn three full days a week. He described how his kids' lives had changed since Jacob started attending the school. He explained how his son first told him about Jacob but failed to mention the simple fact that he was in a wheelchair. It wasn't a detail that struck this child as important.

Cheryl wrote a report that explained how the other kids gravitate toward my son as his wheels cross the threshold of the class each week. She described how Jacob's classmates take turns pushing his wheelchair at recess, reading to him and walking next to him in the hall. She wrote about how kids from other classes come by to say hello. She detailed how his presence in the school transforms the kids from egocentric beings to caring and gentle little people who want to be near Jacob.

And another teacher at Elkhorn, who only knows my son from seeing him in the hallway, wrote the following on our blog in response to my initial article:

I am so glad that you mentioned that everyone benefits from having Jacob at Elkhorn. I do believe children easily embrace differences much more than adults. It is quite disappointing, that in this day and age, we call Jacob's stay at Elkhorn an "unconventional arrangement," when really it should be part of the norm in our school system. Jacob brings just as much positive energy to the children and teachers as he gets in return from them. In the short time Jacob has been at Elkhorn, he has proven that love and friendship can go beyond words. As a teacher, I think this is the best learning that can happen, and I feel honoured that he is a student at my school.

• • •

And so, I persisted. Jacob deserved nothing less from the school board, and he deserved nothing less from me. And on October 23, 2012, he got what he deserved: he was officially registered as an Elkhorn student for three days a week and a Sunny View student for the other two.

"There is a higher court than courts of justice
and that is the court of conscience.
It supercedes all other courts."

Mahatma Gandhi

CHAPTER 9

AND THE VERDICT IS ...

I stood in front of the judge, my entire body trembling, and waited for the questions to begin. After half a day of testimony, I was tired but I was also anxious to get the cross-examination done. The defense attorney, an attractive blonde-haired woman, stood up, smiled and fired a question that hit me so hard I nearly lost my balance: What will you miss most about your son when he's dead?

Andrew and I had filed the lawsuit in 2003, stating that the authors of the article about my family had a duty to inform us about the genetic disorder that they identified in Corey and my grandmother's two sons. The writers were the only ones who had this crucial information and we believed that we should have been told. At the time, the only things I knew about the legal system were from American television shows. But the Canadian judicial system is very different from what we see on *Law and Order*.

Although the case did not come to trial until late in 2009, we had spent years preparing for the event. Unlike our neighbours to the south, Canadians cannot sue for millions of dollars for "pain and suffering." The claim must be based on actual costs involved. Given this stipulation, I had to compile all the receipts related to Jacob's care since his birth, including nursing costs, medical equipment, therapies, diapers—every expense that was associated with caring for our son. This amounted to several binders full of varying sizes of paper. Our claim was based on what we actually spent to care for Jacob, and an actuary was tasked with extrapolating the costs over the course of my son's lifetime.

If the judge ruled in our favour, we would be compensated for the colossal costs of caring for Jacob. We wouldn't be rich, but we would have the funds necessary to provide the ongoing care, equipment and supplies he requires.

• • •

It was a hot and humid day in August 2005 when I first laid eyes on Dr. Gordon Watters, the lead author of the article and the person we held accountable for failing to communicate with my grandmother and Audrey. Andrew, Audrey and I went to Montreal for the discovery phase of the lawsuit. In a large conference room in our lawyer's office, sitting around a formal dining room-length table, we took turns being questioned by Watters' lawyer, and he by ours, to collect the first part of the testimony that would be used to form the basis of each side's legal argument.

Dr. Naomi Fitch, the second author, was not present. She lived in British Columbia and was in the late stages of Alzheimer's disease.

It was tough to sit across the table from the only man in the world who had known—more than thirty years earlier—about the life-changing piece of information contained in my genetic make up. I wanted to lean over the table, look him straight in his eighty-something-year-old eyes and shout, "Why was it more important to you to publish the article than to pick up the phone and warn us? What kind of man can do that?"

But I didn't. I wasn't sure how much restraint I had so I forced myself to look away from him, and I don't know if he looked at me. Our eyes never met.

We were in the room for hours, each one of us questioned "on the record" and "under oath" as a stenographer tapped away at his machine at the head of the table. I was upset that my grandmother, almost ninety years old, was involved in this lawsuit. She was eager to help and willing to do whatever was needed to seek justice, but it must have been so painful for her to revisit such a dark time in her life, reliving the births and deaths of two children, aware that things could have been drastically different for her only granddaughter had we had the elusive bit of information that was so callously withheld from us.

The questions weren't tricky; the goal of the day was to get our stories on file. The lawyers weren't suave like those on TV. They were friendly and asked questions in a clear and straightforward manner. I didn't get the impression that they were trying to trip me up to make me say something that would cause the whole case to be tossed out before it really began. I was nervous but energized because it felt like we were finally moving towards a trial, a chance to right the wrong that we believe was committed against us.

Months went by without news on the pending lawsuit but it was always on my mind, like a little ghost perched on my shoulder whispering in my ear, haunting my thoughts and quiet moments.

Over the next few years, there were times when Andrew and I were asked to provide some information relating to Jacob or our financial situation. We were interviewed by experts on both sides of the case, whose role it was to determine the future cost of care for Jacob. We were subjected to many invasive and insensitive questions around Jacob's symptoms, disease progression and life expectancy.

As heart-wrenching as it was, there was no question that we were going to follow this through to trial. We believed so strongly that we had a right to know about Watters' diagnosis and its implications. We should have been told.

$$\bullet \quad \bullet \quad \bullet$$

The weeks leading up to the trial in December 2009 were peppered with strategy meetings, document reviews and actuarial calculations. Despite all of this, I was still not prepared for the agony of sitting through three weeks of testimony about my son and heartless debates about his anticipated lifespan.

Since we were the plaintiffs, our lawyers presented our case first. Andrew and I were represented by my cousin Arthur, his colleague and the senior partner at their firm. The trial began with an eight-minute video of Jacob—somber images depicting his laboured breathing with tubes taped on his cheek running into his nose as an infant, and progressed to happier scenes of Jacob's face lighting up when he met Andrea Bocelli. I kept my eyes focused on the television, trying to block out the tears running down the court stenographer's cheeks as my son's face flashed across the screen.

The first witness was Jim Garbern, sworn in as one of the world's leading medical experts on PMD. He explained Jacob's disease, along with his current and future symptoms. Over the course of two days he described how PMD worsens as the child ages and stated that there was no cure.

I am fully aware of Jake's symptoms and have an understanding of PMD that is on par with the medical professionals so I know how PMD progresses. Still, as the questions moved to a discussion about how Jacob's disease will ravage his body, I tried to distract myself by doodling on the yellow pad of paper in front of me. I was forced to listen to a conversation about how long Jacob was expected to live—and then, as if that weren't morbid enough, have the defense attorneys argue for an even *shorter* lifespan. The sooner Jacob dies, the defense reasoned, the less money it would cost to care for him. My entire body was trembling. I wanted to stand up and scream at everyone in the room to stop, to put an end to this heartless discussion. Part of me felt like I was betraying my son by being there and by having put the wheels into motion. I couldn't wait to go home and hold Jacob in my arms and kiss his soft cheek.

When it was my turn to testify—at the end of the second day and for most of the third—I was forced to relive the horror of learning that my son had an incurable, devastating disease. I stood in the witness area, in front of a table with a portable tabletop lectern. I discovered that in Canadian courts witnesses stand and we don't get to sit next to the judge. I was positioned with my lawyers seated on my left side and the defense team on my right. I had to describe how my life changed, how the plans and dreams I had were annihilated, and how agonizing it has been to construct a life that is drastically different from what was expected.

There was one positive aspect to my testimony: I was afforded the opportunity to describe my love for my son and acknowledge that Jacob brought joy to my life and taught me a lot about patience and acceptance. I told them that because of Jacob, I witnessed some incredible acts of kindness from people I wouldn't have otherwise met and that despite all the challenges, I felt lucky to be Jacob's mom.

Each day bled into the next, filled with testimony by various experts who argued over whether the authors had had an obligation to inform my family about the genetic mutation.

Both we and the defendants produced witnesses who testified about the equipment Jacob currently uses and would require as he aged. There were debates regarding the type of communication device he would be able to master, whether he would be capable of steering a power wheelchair and whether he would hospitalized for the better part of his last year of life. One of their witnesses made statements about Jacob's abilities after spending less than ten minutes with him, a year earlier, and never having met another PMD patient.

I sat in my assigned seat at the prosecution table, surrounded by piles of thick black binders filled with thousands of pages of legal documents, and fumed. I was livid that someone who had no idea who my son was could stand up and state with conviction that he would never manage a power wheelchair, a skill he practiced every day at school. I clenched my hands so hard that I had nail marks on my palms when I heard her say that Jacob did not have the cognitive ability to learn how to use a computer-assisted communication device, something he was working towards. I wanted to put my head on the table and cry when she stated that Jacob would be so infirm by the time he reached his late teens that he would not require a caregiver at home because he would be spending so much time in the hospital.

There were actuaries who explained, in painstaking detail, the costs that would be associated with caring for Jacob as his disease progressed. The costs of each item—and there were hundreds—were reviewed and cross-examined. Interest rates and depreciation costs and present values were tossed around for several days.

By the end of the trial I was physically drained and emotionally empty. I couldn't stop reliving the questioning and the smell of the courtroom seemed stuck to my skin. Every night when I closed my eyes, I envisioned the attorneys lobbing their questions at each witness.

It took nearly seven years for our case to come to trial, and seven months for the judge to render the judgment we'd been hoping for. In July 2011, we received the 71-page judgment by email.

We won.

The judge found that the doctors should have informed us about their diagnosis. We were entitled to the costs of caring for Jacob and the income I'd lost as a result of being unable to work.

Had this been an episode of *The Good Wife*, the credits would have rolled and the story would have ended. But it wasn't, and it didn't.

Dr. Watters filed an appeal and the horror story continued. In May 2011, the case was heard in the Court of Appeals. It was shortly after Jacob's ninth birthday and eight years after the initial documents were filed.

Unlike the original trial, the Appeal was argued solely by the lawyers in front of three judges, seated next to each other in a row higher than the rest of the courtroom so that everyone had to look up in order to see them. Each side was given a few hours to present its case and no witness testimony was heard. We were informed at the beginning of the day by the sole female judge that everything needed to be wrapped up by the end of the day. No extensions would be given.

Andrew and I sat in the courtroom in the spectator seats since there were no prosecution and defense tables. I glanced across the centre aisle at an older-looking Gordon Watters who stared straight ahead, his gaze never wavering from the front of the room. I wondered how he slept—did he have restful nights, or was he haunted by the fact that he was responsible for withholding crucial information that we could have used to make informed family-planning decisions? I hoped he struggled with that. I believed he deserved to wrestle with those thoughts.

The Appeal process was surreal. The lawyers' arguments were technical in nature, citing prior cases as examples. It was hard for me to follow but we had confidence in our lawyers who were as determined as we were to win this case. I was surprised to see that one of the judges seemed to have trouble concentrating at one point and even appeared to doze off for a bit. But this was our justice system; surely it would work properly, even if one of the judges seemed bored by the discussion. Boy was I naive!

At the conclusion of the day, our three lawyers were confident we would prevail. The only way we would lose, they informed us, was if it was determined that the trial judge made a "palpable" error, one that is clearly wrong or unsupported by the evidence. They believed we would remain victorious.

Eight months later, on a cold Thursday afternoon in February 2012, I was driving to the grocery store when my phone rang around 1:30 p.m. It was Arthur. He received the judgment, he said, and the news wasn't good.

My hands started shaking and I pulled into a parking spot in the first lot I saw. I was floored. I couldn't get my head around what he was saying. Not only did we lose, the new judges had overruled each and every decision made by the trial judge. I don't think I said more than "I can't believe it," over and over. And I know Arthur was equally as stunned.

It took me a few days to summon the fortitude to read through the new judgment, all 41 pages of it. Besides feeling that the decision was so wrong, I kept noticing areas that were factually incorrect. The decision was made based on misinformation. For example, the Appeal court ruled that Dr. Watters did not have to inform us because it would have breeched Corey's confidentiality, but the trial judge stated, in his judgment, that "the doctor never mentioned it as a concern." And the new judgment based the decision on the belief that a doctor was not to be held to the same standard as a "reasonable person," rather the benchmark was what a "reasonable physician" would do in the same situation. The Appeal court did not dispute the trial judge's determination that a "reasonable person" would have informed my grandmother, but unfortunately, the higher court decided that a doctor should be held to a different standard than that of a non-medical professional. I couldn't help thinking that something had gone very awry and that we needed to find a way to rectify it.

So the nightmare continues. We filed a motion to be heard by the Supreme Court of Canada, our last resort, and now we must wait to hear whether the court will listen to our appeal.

In the meantime, the trial continues to haunt me like that little ghost on my shoulder. But I will never forget the moment when the defense attorney stood up and fired that question at me: What would I miss most about Jacob when he was gone? I felt as if I'd been hit with a mallet. I remember noticing her glaring at me. I recall the judge staring at me, waiting for a response, and I remember looking at my lawyers. I pleaded with them with my eyes, asking if I really had to answer that question. The room was silent; everyone was waiting. I had no choice. I took a deep breath and willed my voice to be strong and steady. His smile, I said. I will miss his smile the most.

*"The central struggle of parenthood
is to let our hopes for our children
outweigh our fears."*

Ellen Goodman

CHAPTER 10

A SERIES OF FIRSTS

Jacob clearly has his struggles. Things most people take for granted are impossible for him, including eating, sitting by himself and tossing a ball. Breathing is a challenge and making himself understood is frustrating. Parenting Jake is immensely hard and watching other children thrive sometimes makes me want to run away and hide. And having the lawsuit looming over our heads is a constant reminder that a significant part of our lives is in flux and out of our control.

But despite the hardships, and there are many, Jacob has managed to experience some very typical rites of passage—some "normalcy" among the chaos. And when these moments happen, I feel like jumping up and down, shouting "YES!" and letting everyone know that despite the things he can't do, there are plenty of things he can. Andrew and I long ago resolved to make sure Jacob had as many typical experiences as possible. And we were fortunate enough to stumble into a community of the most accepting, positive and determined girls, girls who opened our eyes to a world of possibilities for our son. Since then, we have learned that with some creativity and planning, there is nothing Jacob can't do.

The first time I saw the flyer for Yedidus in 2005, I asked Jill, Jacob's teacher, about the program. I was told that it was a two-and-a-half-hour program run on Sunday mornings by Orthodox Jewish girls out of Bais Yaakov High School, located a few blocks from our house. It sounded interesting, so I began asking a few more questions. This was the first time I'd come across a program marketed for kids like Jacob, kids with "special needs". He was busy at school from Monday to Friday, but weekends were so long and devoid of activity and stimulation. The information sheet indicated that the children would partake in crafts, music and other hands-on activities. Although the pamphlet was distributed by his school, Jacob's teachers dissuaded me from enrolling in the program. They explained that the lack of adult supervision would expose my son to danger. Their reasoning made sense to me. *Adults* were often afraid to be alone with my son, so I couldn't imagine leaving my defenseless little boy in the care of teenagers some would consider children themselves.

I couldn't have been more wrong, though it would take me another year to figure that out.

When the identical information sheet was distributed the following fall, in September 2006, one of the assistants in Jacob's class asked me if I was going to sign him up for the program. I immediately shook my head and reiterated what I'd been told a year earlier. Hindy vehemently disagreed. She explained that when she was a student at that school, she participated in the program. It was like a weekly camp, with each "camper" paired with a counsellor. The counsellor is educated about the specific needs of the child prior to commencing the program. She volunteered to accompany Jacob to the program until he was comfortable with his counsellor. I wasn't entirely convinced yet, but it was starting to sound like a possibility. Our weekends felt so long; it was hard to find things that Jacob liked to do, or activities he would do with us without screaming.

I agreed to consider it and asked if I could speak to the girls who were running the program.

A few evenings later, my phone rang. On the other end was the excited voice of a young woman who introduced herself as one of the leaders of the Yedidus program. In what I have since learned is the typical speed-talking habit of all her classmates, she explained details about the program. She listed arts and crafts, music, cooking, dancing and colouring as regular activities that the children could engage in. She explained that counsellors helped the kids when they needed it, and that their main goal was to ensure that the campers had a good time.

I described Jacob, his needs and his medical issues. Upon hearing about his feeding tube (and in what struck me as wonderful innocence and a desire to include my son), she exclaimed: "That's okay, I don't get grossed out easily." I had to laugh and admire her willingness to learn how to care for Jake, something most adults I knew were too afraid to do.

I hesitantly agreed to let Jacob try the program—and let the girls try Jacob. True to her word, Hindy met us at the school on the first day and stayed with him during the program. The counsellors were girls dressed in long, black skirts with their hair styled in identical ponytails. They were kids in grades ten through twelve and they ran the program every Sunday morning, when most teenagers were still sleeping, tired from a night out partying with their friends.

As the girls became more confident in lifting and holding Jacob, Hindy backed away and assumed a spectator role. When I returned to check on him, I saw that Jacob was having fun. He was sitting on a counsellor's lap and enjoying the singing and dancing around him. I relaxed slightly, and knowing I lived only a few blocks away, I agreed to enroll my son in the program.

Looking back on it now, I did the right thing. I learned that the Orthodox Jewish community gives its children more responsibilities at an earlier age than those who lead a secular life. They marry younger, have children younger, and are taught to be charitable, financially as well as with their time, at a much younger age. A sixteen-year-old in the Orthodox Jewish community is much more responsible and more interested in helping a neighbour than a typical teenager, who is likely more concerned with the hottest music and latest fashion trends.

The first time I'd consciously noticed the figures in black was when I was a child going to the bagel factory with my parents on a Saturday night in Montreal. The bagels were hot; the car windows would fog up during our drive home and the interior was rich with the aroma of warm bread and sesame seeds. I remember watching the men dressed in black suits and black hats, even during the hottest nights of July.

Following a short distance behind these shadowy figures were the women, wearing shirts with long sleeves and long skirts, pushing baby strollers, older children holding the hands of their younger siblings. I watched these people and wondered why they chose to have so many children, and why the women agreed to wear wigs. I thought about how awful it must be for the children to be raised without television.

When I was younger I thought I knew so many things about these religious Jews. I knew all about them despite never having spoken to a single member. I knew they lived in Outremont. I knew they took the bus to New York after sundown on Saturday nights. I knew they believed it was important to study the Torah. And I was convinced that they would not consider me Jewish because my beliefs and practices were so different from theirs. And I was wrong. So wrong. It would take years and painful experiences for me to learn that my understanding of this group was inaccurate. Completely inaccurate.

•   •   •

Not only did Jacob now have a weekend activity to look forward to, but he met some wonderfully caring girls who fell in love with him. Some of the most phenomenal examples of compassion and love are showered on Jacob when these kids play with him, talk to him and spin him in circles to make him laugh. These girls, who dress in skirts that fall four inches below their knees, help reinforce Jacob's younger sisters' belief that princesses only wear skirts.

Jacob is a fixture at Bais Yaakov on Sundays and is adored by almost all the students at the school. At 10:30 on Sunday mornings, as I push his wheelchair into the driveway of the school, Jacob starts squirming. His obvious excitement when he realizes where we are is restrained only by the seatbelt and foot straps that secure his body to his chair. The chorus of high-pitched "hi Jacobs!" erupts as soon as the first teenager spots us. As we enter the building, a demurely clad counsellor affectionately whisks Jacob out of my arms and plants kisses on his cheeks.

Bracha, Jacob's counsellor during his first year at Yedidus and his favourite person in the world, saw Jacob at his best and at his worst. Just mentioning her name made him smile. Hearing her raspy voice on the telephone was enough to stop him from screaming, regardless of the initial cause of upset. She witnessed Jacob's choking episodes, seizures, hives, general discomfort and more than one episode of projectile vomiting. She was extremely capable with Jacob, so much so that I often forgot she was a teenager.

Some of our family and friends shook their heads in disbelief (or was it disapproval?) when they heard we had no qualms about entrusting Jacob's well-being to this group of girls. They looked surprised (or was it shocked?) that these kids knew how to feed him through the tube in his stomach. I can only imagine how irresponsible they considered me to be when they learned about The Sleepover.

· · ·

Jacob has few friends his own age. But Taryn, a girl ten days his junior, is Jake's girlfriend. Smarter than most kids her age, at five years old Taryn's special talent was identifying whether a word was a preposition, adjective or adverb. Nouns were too easy. During the summer of 2007, a few days into the August session at camp, I was told by Jake's shadow, the woman who stays by Jake's side and helps him participate in all the activities with his able-bodied bunkmates, that Jacob had made a new friend. Taryn innocently described Jacob to her mom, saying that he was in a stroller, he can't speak or eat, but he likes it when she kisses his eyeballs.

A few days later, Taryn announced that Jacob was her new "number 1 best friend." By the following week, Jacob was Taryn's boyfriend. At five years old, this little girl wasted no time getting to know him. This incredible blond-haired girl with deep dimples on both cheeks donates all her tooth fairy money to PMD research so she can help find a cure for Jake's disease. Jacob cracks up with laughter when she leans over to kiss his eyeballs.

Another friend is Harry, a little boy who attends the same school as my son. Like Jacob, Harry is in a wheelchair and cannot speak. When both boys are placed on a mat on the floor, they hold hands and laugh together. When Harry's name is mentioned at home, Jacob grins.

But the majority of Jacob's friends are older girls from Bais Yaakov High School, affectionately known as Jacob's Princesses. These girls take turns holding my son and dancing with him. They complain about "Jacob withdrawal" if they don't see him for a week. So when Batsheva invited him over for a sleepover at her house, I immediately said yes.

Jacob was seven years old when he had his first sleepover. It was at a girl's house. Her parents were away for the weekend and he had a great time.

Late Friday afternoon in the winter of 2009, with Jake's clothes, medications and liquid nutrition packed, his wheelchair and IV pole crammed in the back of the van, we set off for his latest adventure. During the car ride to his friend's house, I explained to my son that he was going to stay there for Shabbat (the Jewish Sabbath, which runs from sundown Friday until after sundown on Saturday) and that I would come pick him up the following evening. The smile on his face assured me that he was excited about this new experience. As I carried him into Batsheva's house, her warm embrace welcomed Jacob and allowed me to leave without a murmur of protest from my son.

Back at home, my house seemed different. It was quieter without Jacob. With both my daughters in bed by eight o'clock I realized that this was the first time since Jacob's birth that I would be able to lounge around in my pajamas before going to bed. Emily, Jake's night nurse, would not be arriving at 11:30 to tend to Jacob's needs during the night. This would be the first time in almost eight years that my entire household was asleep at the same time. It was a normal situation for most families, but felt strange and unsettling to me.

The next morning was surreal. My typical Saturday craziness begins at 9 a.m., when Emily leaves. Within minutes, Jake is screaming and everyone is hustled into the car for a few hours of driving and time-wasting errands to Home Depot or Wal-Mart, until it is time for all the kids' swimming lessons. This particular Saturday was more serene. We stayed in bed and watched cartoons on television until mid-morning and gradually made our way to the pool in time for the lesson. It was a pleasant way to start the weekend.

But on some level, it didn't feel right. Jacob wasn't with us.

As the day went on, I noticed how quiet my house was. I wasn't glued to the clock to make sure I didn't miss a medication dose or run out of bibs for my chronic drooler. There was an element of tranquility in my home, a word that isn't usually used to describe our abode. But the calmer my life became, the more agitated I felt.

My mind kept drifting to thoughts of my son. I wondered if Jakey was having fun and what he was doing. Because he was celebrating Shabbat with his friends and the Sabbath rules dictate that they cannot use the telephone, I was unable to get an update. As much as I wanted to, I could not get in touch with him, short of showing up unannounced at Batsheva's house. I reassured myself that he was in capable hands and that if something terrible happened, surely I would be notified. I felt helpless and nervous and unsettled, but I tried to be strong so that Jacob could have this incredible experience.

At 7 p.m. on the dot I went to pick up Jacob. As I hurried up the front stairs and waited at the door, my heart pounded with apprehension. Questions were swarming around my brain: Had he been able to sleep in a new bed? Had he woken up scared and unsure of where he was? How was his day?

When the door opened and I saw my gap-toothed son sitting in his wheelchair in the middle of the living room, my racing heart slowed. When I was close enough to ruffle his thick hair and give him a big hug, I knew that he'd had a wonderful time.

My son had had a sleepover at a friend's house! He'd had a fantastic time and by all accounts did not miss his mom. I, on the other hand, missed him terribly. But despite my internal struggle with his absence, I know I did the right thing in letting him go. Jacob's many medical issues make his life more challenging than most, but he deserves to have regular childhood experiences and I'd long ago vowed to do whatever I could to facilitate them.

• • •

My ability to keep that promise was tested a few months later when the summer arrived and the school year ended.

"Have you lost your mind?" Megan shrieked into the phone after I told her about Jacob's summer plans. My friend did not attempt to hide her disapproval, which was only heightened when I told her that three teenagers would be responsible for his well-being.

Maybe I had lost it. In the face of Megan's shock, I felt deeply unsure about my decision and I started doubting my parental abilities, again.

As the parent of a child who cannot speak or move independently, I asked myself if it was irresponsible of me to send him to an overnight camp, in a neighbouring province, with teenaged caregivers whose lifestyle and beliefs are different from mine?

But the decision was made. During the week prior to Jacob's departure, with all his clothes scattered in piles on his bed and across the floor, I packed for my seven-year-old son's upcoming adventure. I did all the things necessary to ensure his readiness for overnight camp. There were t-shirts and shorts, long-sleeved tops and pants, bathing suits and pajamas in his duffel bag.

It was a typical pre-camp scene, one that many people were enacting at the same time during the last few weeks of June. But this scenario was different from that of our neighbours. In addition to stuffing his blue bag full of clothes and bedding, I methodically packed a second bag with syringes, feeding tubes and the various medications that Jake needs every four hours around the clock.

When asked by friends if I was worried about sending Jacob away for three weeks, I emphatically told them that he would be well cared for and that I was confident this would be a great experience for him. I ignored the queasiness in the pit of my stomach that surfaced every time I thought about it. Was sending my disabled child to camp, whose needs are complex and constant, the action of a responsible parent?

• • •

Jacob has an ability to make people fall in love with him. There is something intangible that draws people to him and makes them want to be near him, help him and laugh with him.

Jacob's people-magnet skills first surfaced during that prolonged hospital stay following his birth. The nurses would argue over who would have him on their charge list for the day. Our morning would begin with the lucky winner entering his room with a smile, ready to start his daily routine of medication administration.

Bracha, Jacob's favourite princess—and yet another person he'd managed to charm—convinced me to send Jacob to Camp Yaldei, a camp for children with special needs, located in the Laurentian Mountains in Quebec, an eight-hour drive from our home. At Yaldei, Jacob would have the opportunity to go swimming, boating, participate in arts and crafts, baking, music, day trips and theme days, just like his typical peers would in a regular overnight camp. She selected two other princesses to accompany them. The three girls were breathless with excitement as they unveiled their plan – Bracha would be with him during the day, and Batsheva and Shoshana would be responsible for his overnight care.

We arrived at camp in the evening, two minutes before a thunderstorm. As the car slowed to a stop, my heart was beating quickly and my breath was shallow. It was really happening: Jacob was going to stay at camp without me for three weeks. Until then, the longest I had been without Jacob was twenty-four hours, the time he spent at Batsheva's for his overnight experience.

An hour later, Jacob was sleeping soundly in what was affectionately labeled "Jacob's Palace" because of the coloured-pencil drawing affixed to the outside of his bedroom. Inside his room, there were more handmade signs and pictures taped on the walls. Batsheva and Shoshana, who had been at camp for a few days prior to our arrival, drew pictures of Jacob, wrote his name in bubble letters and taped them to the wall above his bed.

Unlike my son, I was not relaxed. Not at all. I was unpacking his medical paraphernalia and anxiously trying to share as much information as possible with the camp nurse, a woman exhausted from a long first day of camp. The refrigerator, necessary for Jacob's food and medications, was not in the prearranged spot. We were unable to locate electrical sockets in his room to plug in his nebulizer, a device needed to administer one of his medications.

After some running around on the part of the counsellors, things started coming together. With a few final reassurances from the camp directors that he would be safe, I reluctantly left my little boy in the able care of his doting princesses.

Happy and excited for Jacob to have this experience, I was also nervous. I remember the first time I went to overnight camp—I was eight years old, a year older than Jacob. Every once in a while, I wondered whether he was too young for this but I quickly pushed those thoughts out of my head. I knew Jacob was with people who loved him and were well-trained in his care. And there was a nurse on site at all times. Nevertheless, Andrew and I were reluctant to drive back to Toronto so we decided to stay with my parents in Montreal. We reasoned that the ninety-minute drive from Montreal to camp was preferable to the eight hours from Toronto in the case of an emergency. Andrew was able to work remotely, and Sierra and Jamie would have the opportunity to spend three weeks with their grandparents. It was a perfect solution.

When I was a camper, there was no such thing as email. My parents depended on my letters, handwritten and sealed in a pre-addressed, stamped envelopes and sent via "snail mail" to find out what I was doing at camp. I don't know how they, and everyone else back then, didn't flood the camp office with daily phone calls! Thankfully, Bracha sent me frequent updates and emailed photos. I took great comfort in her few words, just knowing he was healthy and having so much fun. And once a week, on Friday afternoon, Bracha would call me and hold the phone next to Jake's ear so I could hear his voice and tell him I loved him.

Daily reports from Bracha were constantly positive: "Jacob had fun boating today." "Your son is dangerously cute and had an awesome time on the trampoline." And my favourite: "He's my best friend in the whole world!"

Not content to rely solely on Bracha's updates, we visited Jacob partway through his camp session. As Andrew, Sierra, Jamie and I walked across the lawn to the building where Jacob was, several counsellors came up to us and gushed about how much they loved our son and how much fun they were having playing with him.

Jacob was wheeled to me flanked by five caring counsellors and his new friend, Nosson, the nine-year-old son of the camp director. As soon as I saw Jake, I knew he was in his element: his huge gap-toothed smile was all the convincing I needed.

We toured the camp and met his princesses, whose number had grown exponentially. Jacob looked tanned, healthy and ecstatic. I was so proud of my little guy, and all the tension I had inside my gut evaporated.

He was excited to see me, as evidenced by the wet, sloppy kisses he kept giving me, but he was not ready to come home. As I was leaving, I asked if he wanted to come with me, to which he quickly vocalized, his way of saying "No!" When I asked if he wanted to stay with his princesses, he didn't hesitate and immediately nodded his head "Yes." After a few more hugs and kisses, I drove away with a sense of calm that had eluded me since the night we brought him to camp.

The following June, when Jacob's clothes and medications were once again laid out on his bed, ready to be packed for a return trip to camp, I recalled his beaming smile and high-pitched squeal when I'd visited him the previous summer. I have no doubt that I did the right thing for him and I know that Jacob had the time of his life at camp. What more could I want for my son? What more could any parent want?

•   •   •

It has been five years since Jacob began attending Yedidus. Five years since my family was enveloped by a group of intelligent, sensitive and fun girls. They possess a maturity and empathy that continues to astound and impress me. These girls are constantly trying to find ways to help us by taking care of Jacob if his caregiver is away, offering to pick up groceries and inviting him to their homes to help them light Chanukah candles and sing songs.

If someone had told me, fifteen years ago, that in 2011 I would be the mother of three children, one of whom had a severe disability whose care was so consuming that I wouldn't be able to return to work, I would have thought it impossible. If the same person had told me that I would be dependent on the assistance and generosity of others on a daily basis, I would have screamed in horror. And if that person mentioned that I would be happy, I would have started looking for the hidden camera that a jokester had placed nearby to capture my reactions to this ludicrous story.

The crazy thing is that it's true. All of it. My successful career was sidelined the day I gave birth to my first child. And my natural instinct to "do it all" was rocked to the core. How would I, an independent, successful woman in the investment industry, learn to depend on the assistance of others without feeling like a complete failure? I never expected to be dependent on other people but I am. Not by choice, but by necessity. And out of this necessity, I have managed to create a great group of friends for my son, even though our reality does not match the picture I'd envisioned all those years ago. The adage that it takes a village to raise a child is the philosophy I live by. And both Jacob and I are stronger for being part of this remarkable village.

Jacob, age 4

— MARCH 2006 —

"You've developed the strength of a draft horse while holding onto the delicacy of a daffodil ... you are the mother, advocate and protector of a child with a disability."

Lori Borgman

CHAPTER 11

YES HE CAN

Over the course of Jacob's lifetime, I have encountered all sorts of people in positions of authority: professionals at school, in hospitals and at camp. Everyone has a different reaction when they meet my son, ranging from complete acceptance to hesitation to fear, and all stops in between.

Being a parent of a severely disabled child is indescribably difficult and it presents so many challenges, not the least of which is a constant battle against fear borne out of ignorance. But there is no reason to be scared of my son. His disability is not contagious, though his laughter is. And it is so hard to deal with people who don't understand that.

Around the time that most new mothers are starting to feel comfortable with their bundles of joy, I was thrust into the terrifying and unexpected role of protector—not in the typical "I won't let anyone push you in the playground" way. I was learning to stand up to ignorant people, people who were afraid of my son.

I am not naive enough to believe that everyone must accept my child without hesitation. He is different. He can't sit by himself, he drools and, although he understands everything that goes on around him, his communication skills are very limited.

It's not easy to look at this beautiful little boy—with his thick dark hair, sparkling green eyes, and a giggle that makes you want to laugh too—in a body that doesn't work properly.

But when someone takes the time to come close and look a bit deeper, they can see so much life and mischief in those gigantic green eyes (lined with enviously long black eyelashes!).

I have learned that young children, especially, are incredibly accepting of differences. When he was three, Jacob attended a summer camp with "regular" kids. Although his bunkmates understood he was different — he couldn't walk, talk or eat like they did — he still fit in. When the group participated in a scavenger hunt, some kids helped him collect his pieces without a counsellor's prompting.

At the end of another summer camp experience, the director called to tell me she thought the staff and other campers benefited at least as much from being around Jacob as he did from being at camp. She told me that a group of children would take turns sitting next to him, recording their voices on his communication switch, which he uses to make himself understood, and reading to him after lunch. I was not surprised, but I was proud of my son.

And there's his ongoing friendship with Taryn. Jacob and Taryn are both ten years old now and continue to share a special friendship. And I love that Taryn can see beyond Jacob's PMD and his challenges.

Jacob's experience with typically developing kids has always been positive — young children tend to gravitate toward him, not savvy enough to notice their parents' discomfort over how to react in the presence of a severely disabled child.

I do not know a single person who would say their child has been negatively affected by my son. But I can list many people who would say their lives have been sweetened by spending time with Jacob and watching their children make him laugh his contagious laugh.

As an observer, it angers me to watch a professional ignore my son and pretend he isn't in the room, or look away when it is clear that Jacob requires a new bib or a clean shirt.

But sometimes people who choose to work with Jacob need time to get over the fear of interacting with him. It took many months for one of his teachers, for example, to realize that she could touch him without hurting him, and that changing his bib wouldn't cause him to break.

When Jacob was eight years old, I visited his classroom unannounced. I had an appointment at the school with his occupational therapist and a vendor to look at a new wheelchair. The teacher didn't know I was coming and she certainly wasn't expecting me to enter the classroom at that time. When his teacher heard my gasp from the other end of the classroom, she immediately came running over. The first words out of her mouth were, "I know what it looks like but it's only been a minute," as if that was going to make everything all right and erase the image of indignity from my mind.

Jacob was in the middle of the room, facing the wall and isolated from the other children who were grouped around a table engaged in the day's lesson with the teacher. I was mortified. My son was alone, without a book, toy or anything to arouse his interest. He was slumped in his chair. The bandana around his neck was drenched with drool and his feeding pump was beeping incessantly. It was as if the educator had separated him from his peers because she was afraid the beeping was a prelude to an explosion. I am still at a loss to explain why his bib was so wet and had not been changed earlier. I was fuming, furious at the instructor and the assistants for showing him such disrespect and achingly sad for Jacob's inability to advocate on his own behalf. I immediately stripped off his soiled

shirt and replaced it with the dry one that was in the bag attached
to his wheelchair, along with a seemingly endless supply of clean
bandanas.

Jacob's inability to speak is one of the worst aspects of his PMD.
Jacob understands so much! I can't even imagine how exasperating
it must be for him to want to say, "this is what I want" and despite
repeated attempts at communicating, have his desires remain
undeciphered.

I desperately want to get inside my son's head and hear what
he is thinking, what he wants and how I can make things better for
him. I long to have a discussion about something that interests him
and listen to him express the ideas he has built up over the course of
his lifetime. I dream of my son being able to tell me why he screams
unrelentingly the moment the nurse leaves on the weekend. If I
knew why he yells, maybe I could help him get what he needs and
make both our lives a bit calmer.

But that day when I walked into his classroom unexpectedly,
a realization smacked me right in the face: there is another side to
Jacob's inability to articulate his thoughts. Because he can't speak,
he cannot tell me things I should know, things that are wrong that
I might be able to help him fix, or fix for him. If his teachers don't
write about it in his book, I don't learn that Jacob's ankle braces are
uncomfortable and need to be replaced; I am unaware that a teacher
is talking about bringing her dog to school; and I don't know that
his teacher seems so scared of hurting Jacob that she won't change
his bib, even if it is in dire need of replacing.

The indignity that I witnessed horrified me. Although his
teacher had not intended to insult Jacob in this way, she realized
how inappropriate her actions were as soon as she saw me in the

room. Had I not entered at that moment, I would not have known the seclusion and neglect that Jacob was subject to. It wouldn't have been reported in his communication book and he certainly would not have shared the details with me later at home. I can't help but wonder what else goes unnoticed or unspoken during Jacob's day. How many times does he get pushed aside or forgotten because he can't stand up for himself?

· · ·

Several months later, Jacob and I were at his school, waiting for the orthotist to bring him the new pair of ankle-foot-orthotics (AFOs), similar to leg braces that we'd had made a few weeks earlier. I was engaged in a conversation with Jake's physiotherapist, Nancy, the woman who'd prescribed his latest piece of equipment. Nancy was sitting on one side of Jacob and I was on the other, my arm slung across Jacob's thin shoulders.

Out of the corner of my eye, I saw a stranger pull up a chair and sit at Jacob's feet. She proceeded to take his right leg in her hands and started to remove his socks. Surprised and offended that someone would invade my son's personal space by touching him without requesting permission to do so, I blurted out a curt-sounding: "Who are you and what are you doing?"

Before Jacob was born I did not give much thought to how to treat a person who was different. My only experience with degenerative illness was with my grandfather's youngest brother. Uncle Ruby had Parkinson's disease and by the time I was born he walked with a cane, had tremors in his hands and his speech was hard to comprehend. I wasn't scared of him, though. In fact, he was my favourite uncle. Whenever I was able to choose a topic for a school project, I invariably selected Parkinson's disease.

I was in my early teens when I learned that just because the outside of person looks broken, it doesn't necessarily follow that their brain is broken too. I had no idea at the time how well that profound lesson would serve me years later. During one of his hospitalizations, Uncle Ruby was weaned off all his medications prior to a procedure. I can still recall my mother describing her visit with him. She was astounded when she walked into his hospital room and he greeted her with a clearly audible "hello, Bev." She was even more surprised when she had a real conversation with him, the first in many years. Apparently, a side effect of one of his medications was slurred speech. When he wasn't taking the medication, it was obvious that his mind was clear, and he proved it by remembering her birthdate, stating it in the context of the conversation they were having.

When Jacob was first diagnosed with PMD, I read as many descriptions of the disease as I could find. Most stated that the patient's physical impairments are much greater than his cognitive impairments. At the time, it was too early to know if this would be true for Jacob, but by the time he was a few years old, it was clear to all those who interacted with him that he understood a lot more than people realized. He listened intently to adult conversations and laughed appropriately at the punch lines of jokes.

I recognize that people assume that because Jacob cannot move independently and can't speak, that he can't comprehend what is being said to and around him. But I won't accept that ignorance and I won't sit back and let that misconception stand.

So when the orthotist began her exam of Jacob without asking his permission, I barked at her to stop. Startled, she dropped Jacob's foot, albeit gently, stammered her name and apologized.

She explained that she had jumped in and started the appointment without an introduction because Nancy and I were engaged in a conversation that she did not want to interrupt. Her intentions were good but her courtesy was directed at the wrong people. Jacob, the patient, should have been the target of her affability.

There is a fine line between standing up for Jacob with the intention of getting him what he deserves and offending the person responsible for giving it to him. And I am sometimes guilty of crossing the line in my protective attempt to advocate for my non-verbal son. But I'd rather risk coming off too strong to a stranger than letting my son feel like he shouldn't be treated as the intelligent person that he is.

I can't be at my son's side all the time, but I wish I could. I want to be his voice and refuse to let him be cast aside because his machine beeps when it's empty or because his bibs need replacing every ten minutes. He deserves to be treated with respect and dignity. If he could speak, I know he would agree.

Once in a while, something special happens and Jacob and I encounter acts of incredible decency and compassion. Often, these people don't realize how their actions affect us. It's those select moments that make me appreciate how the simple act of speaking directly to my son—instead of through me, or instead of ignoring him completely—can make me so happy.

One of the best examples came when I took then eight-year-old Jacob to the dentist. His appointment was the last one of the day, at 3:30. From the moment I'd woken up that morning, I'd felt a ball of dread bouncing around my stomach.

Taking Jacob to any appointment is an ordeal. Physically, it is difficult for me to carry him into the car. There is a lot to remember to bring with us, including bibs, a change of clothing, diapers and depending on the time of day, pre-measured medication loaded into syringes, his food and his feeding pump. Emotionally, medical appointments are challenging because Jacob hates being examined. He yells, his only way to protest, for the entire duration of the meeting.

As much as I tried to put the day's consultation out of my mind, it kept popping back into my consciousness and I imagined the sound of Jacob's angry screams reverberating in my ears.

His school bus arrived home at the usual time, 3:10 p.m. I immediately placed him into his car seat and clumsily heaved his one-hundred-plus-pound wheelchair into the back of my van. During the fifteen-minute car ride, I told him where we were headed and reminded him that he was a big boy and didn't need to be scared.

I explained to Jacob that we were going to a new dentist because it was the same dentist his sisters go to. Sierra and Jamie really like him and we thought Jacob would like him too.

Given that Jacob is fed by a tube inserted directly into his stomach and that his teeth have never come in contact with food, one would think that dentist visits are not necessary. Ironically, that is not the case. The act of chewing functions to clean teeth, in much the same way as a toothbrush does. Because Jacob doesn't chew, plaque accumulates in his mouth at a much faster rate and he needs a dental exam every four months.

Until that day, Jacob had always gone to the same dentist, an experienced professional who rarely spoke directly to him. My son's typical behavioural pattern was to start screaming uncontrollably the second his wheels crossed the threshold of the exam room.

Jacob's screams are incessant and leave him soaked in sweat, making it appear as if he has just emerged from a shower. When in the midst of a screaming session, he also chokes, due to the fact that he cannot swallow all the secretions that his yelling causes. In short, the dentist visit is torturous for all involved, but it's especially hellish for Jacob.

Sadly, most of the medical professionals we've encountered over the years have had virtually no social interaction with him. One of the worst instances where Jacob the person was ignored was during an appointment to have his G-tube changed. My son lay on a hard, cold table underneath a giant x-ray machine. He was screaming, probably because he was scared and was being restrained by nurses whose faces were covered with the standard-issue hospital masks. I was by his side, trying to comfort him, when a man walked up to Jacob and proceeded to rip the tape that held the G-tube in place off Jake's belly. Enraged, I stepped in front of him and asked who he was and what was he doing. Without missing a beat, he stated his name, emphasizing the prefix "Doctor." I replied that I would like him to introduce himself to his patient before beginning what was clearly an upsetting procedure. Many years later, I am still disgusted with this physician who had no regard for Jacob as a person, and I am so glad that I was there to be Jacob's voice once again.

I cringe each time a doctor ignores my son and speaks only to me. Even when I inform them that Jacob understands our conversation, they don't interact with him. They often begin their examination without asking Jacob's permission to touch him or explaining what they will do.

I didn't expect today's dentist appointment to be any different.

As we entered the small, non-air-conditioned office we were told that the dentist would see us shortly. I wheeled Jacob into the waiting room and banged into a chair along the way because the aisle was not wide enough for Jake's wheels to pass easily. I sat down next to my son and reminded him what would happen during the appointment. A few times his mouth contorted into a sad frown that made me want to cry, but Jacob was able to compose himself. He was trying to be brave.

The room was hot and stuffy and I worried that the temperature alone would upset him. A friendly hygienist came up to us, crouched down and told Jacob that it wouldn't be much longer until it was his turn. Jacob looked at her and listened while she spoke to him. I just stared in disbelief: I couldn't remember the last time someone at an appointment had thought to bend down and speak directly to my son. This simple act of conversing with Jacob, at his eye level, was enough to make me notice that so far this appointment was different from most others we've been to.

A short while later, the dentist, a tall, lanky man with a big smile, walked into the room and promptly shook Jacob's hand. "Hi Jacob," he said, "my name is Ed." Instead of breaking into an ear-piercing shriek at the sight of this stranger, Jacob lifted his head to look at the newcomer. He was curious and willing to let this person speak to him. Ed sat down on his stool and explained, to Jacob, what he wanted to do during the appointment. He then asked Jacob if it was okay with him. It turns out that treating Jacob like a person was all it took for him to listen and not scream. When it came time for the actual exam, my son was calm and co-operative.

As I watched this interaction unfold, I felt my heart was racing. I was amazed by Jacob's behaviour. I couldn't believe this was the same kid whose screams had become legendary at the hospital where we attend most of our appointments. I was so proud of my son and I felt like giving the dentist a huge hug. I tried explaining to him how dramatically different Jake's behaviour was and how talking directly to him made such a difference. I don't think Ed fully understood the magnitude of this event and how it altered things for us.

Later that night, when I replayed the afternoon in my head, I felt a heavy sadness in my chest. I realized that during all the previous appointments Jacob was probably screaming for someone to explain what they wanted from him, or simply what they were going to do. It was terribly distressing to me that it had taken eight years to find someone who was willing to look past Jacob's physical impairments to see the *person* in the wheelchair. I imagined how different the past eight years of appointments would have been if the doctors who had ignored my son had been open to treating the whole person he is and not just whatever body part concerned them.

Since that momentous day, both Jacob and I have changed. At the start of our meetings, I mention to the professional that Jacob does not like being examined and that doctors scare him. I explain that if they speak to him and explain what will happen, he might be more co-operative. So far, it's worked. Appointments are still physically difficult, but they are not as terrible as they once were.

"A person's a person, no matter how small."

Dr. Seuss

CHAPTER 12

IT'S NEVER ENOUGH

Jacob is amazing and I adore him. There is nothing I wouldn't do for him. But being his mother can be so hard at times—emotionally draining and physically exhausting. And I never feel like I'm doing enough. I always think I can do more. When a new idea comes to mind, I berate myself for not thinking of it sooner. Because small things can have a huge impact on Jacob's life and a few months can make a difference. Maybe.

When Jacob was younger, I diligently dragged him to various therapy appointments. I held out hope that someone would teach him to walk, play with a toy or eat. If physiotherapy was prescribed twice a week, I wanted him to go four times. Whatever therapies he received at Zareinu, I supplemented with extra sessions after school.

As Jacob grew and it became clear that the therapies were having minimal effect, I eventually loosened my compulsion to make sure his schedule was packed with people who could teach him to sit, swallow or move. It took time, but I learned to accept that the therapies wouldn't stop his disease from progressing. And the fact that he detested some of his therapists and would choke on their tables (as a result of all his screaming) helped convince me to let go.

But I have never abandoned my quest to ensure that Jacob continues to thrive. I am weighed down by the pressure I put on myself, angry when I realize I might have missed an opportunity to make Jake's life a little easier or better – like, for example, when it suddenly dawned on me that he lacks the tools needed to ask a question.

Jacob has never asked me a question. He is a child and all children are curious beings. From the moment my daughters could speak, they asked thousands of questions, ranging from the simple "when will you be home?" to the more profound "what is PMD?"

It wasn't as if Jacob's communication issues weren't on my mind. For years, I had been focused on finding a way for Jacob to "speak," to be able to communicate what he's thinking. And with the help of some remarkable people, I succeeded. Jacob's adapted iPod has finally given him a voice. Using a switch positioned near his cheek, he can push the button to select from several pre-recorded messages, including "I want to sit on your lap," "I want to read a story," and "I am uncomfortable, please change my position." But something was missing—something important—and I didn't realize it until recently. There are no questions in Jacob's list of pre-recorded messages, no way for him to indicate that he might want more information, clarification or a more in-depth explanation. I'm incensed at myself for failing to notice this gap sooner.

Those who know Jacob are well aware of his intelligence and his capacity to understand and react to conversations. He's a smart kid, and I've always known he has a lot to say. But he probably has a lot of questions too.

One evening last year, I returned from an incomplete family vacation with Andrew and our daughters (Jacob's medical issues make it impossible for him to travel with us). Our taxi pulled into the driveway just after 8 p.m. and I was hoping to spend time with Jacob before he fell asleep. I was excited to see him.

I dropped the car seats and knapsack at the foot of the stairs and ran up to greet him. Jake was already in bed, his hair still wet from his shower. His meal was hooked up to his feeding tube and dripping slowly into his belly. I crawled onto his bed behind him and gave my son a big hug. It took him a few seconds to process what was happening, but when he realized it was me he let out an excited squeal and wiggled his legs. I removed the pillows that are used to prop him on his side and keep his hips level, turned him over to face me, gave him a big kiss on his cheek, and whispered that I was so happy to see him. It was obvious by his reaction that he was happy too.

Then I started peppering him with questions: Did he have fun while we were away? Did he enjoy his sleepover at Bracha's house? Did he miss us? He responded to each inquiry, nodding his head to indicate yes and vocalizing for no, moving the discussion along. Typical of many kids his age, he gave the biggest "yes" when I asked if he wanted a present.

A short while later, all the kids were asleep and the house was quiet. But my mind wasn't. I mulled over all the things Jacob probably wanted to tell me but couldn't. I wanted to hear about how school had been during the week we were away, if he'd had fun at his program on the weekend and what he'd liked most about his sleepover. And I wondered what he felt when the four of us headed to the airport and he stayed behind. This thought pattern wasn't new—I often find myself thinking these things. Still, it is painful and I try not to dwell on it. Sometimes I am more successful than others.

On that particular night, it was as if a light bulb suddenly turned on in my head. Questions! I ask Jacob a slew of them every day but he has never asked me a single one. He can't. He doesn't have the tools to do so. And here I was, eight-and-a-half years into his life, just figuring this out. It was as if all the air was knocked out of me. I slumped lower in my chair as I started to process this new information. How had I missed it? Was this another source of frustration for my son, one that he wanted to share but couldn't?

Research shows that children are inquisitive and learn by asking questions. They also soak up information by exploring, touching and playing. Jacob can't do any of these things on his own yet he loves to learn. The more I think about this, the heavier my heart feels. Ever since he was four and had a teacher who took the time to really teach and test Jacob on the material she presented, it has been clear that he hungers for information. And we have to give it to him; he can't seek it out on his own.

Educators have told me that we need to expose Jacob to different sensations: hot and cold, hard and soft, furry and slimy. We need to rub his hands and feet on a variety of materials so that he can process their differences. I know how to help him play, using hand-over-hand, modified games and other creative methods to allow him to explore, grasp the concept of cause and effect, and learn how things work.

I ask a lot of questions; it helps me clarify whatever concept happens to be under discussion. I have difficulty following the conversation when my understanding is muddled. A few simple queries can have a tremendous benefit in helping me stay focused on the matter. But Jacob lacks these simple tools. I am astounded at the patience he has cultivated, patience that allows him to listen and not raise his hand or blurt out an inquiry because he physically cannot do it. Despite the frustration he must experience each time he wants to ask something, he still manages to learn. I am fascinated by my son.

Whether Jacob's lack of ability to ask questions was simply an oversight on the part of the educators and therapists or a situation that was just too complicated to remedy is unclear to me. But I can't get it out of my mind. It makes me want to weep. I have to figure out how to help him cultivate this skill.

And it's not the only thing that weighs heavy on my mind. Another struggle is finding things to do with Jake that he enjoys. I have tried so many things, including books on tape, walks and adapted basketball, to name a few. Sometimes I drag him along with me on errands, like grocery shopping, because I want to spend time with my son.

As Jacob and I make our way down the crowded aisles in the produce section, I am acutely aware of strangers glancing at us. They see a mother and son shopping together. But we stand out because we are different.

Because Jacob can't sit or stand without support, I cannot secure him in the seat at the front of the cart or have him stand at the end, holding on to the metal basket as I push a food-filled wagon through the store. Instead, we make our way down the aisle with me pushing him in his wheelchair and him balancing our selected items on his lap.

Like many kids his age, Jacob does not enjoy this errand. As soon I stop pushing him to grab an item off the shelf, he complains. Jacob knows what he wants, but unlike his peers he can't run ahead and explore on his own. This frustrates him, so he screams. As I try to console him, he screams louder.

While many parents can treat their little helpers to a candy or bag of chips at the end of a shopping expedition, I do not have the luxury of this reward at my disposal. And so the screaming continues and eventually escalates.

Moments like this are particularly trying. Ever since Jacob was born, he has had a special effect on people. Year after year, I have watched my son attract people to him and melt their hearts with his infectious laughter and mischievous grin.

But when they leave, he changes. He screams, he protests and he cries. Gone is the charm, the loveable smile and the twinkle in his green eyes. I am left with an angry, inconsolable little boy. And this is when I start to ask myself a hard question: Why can't I elicit the same wonderful qualities that his nurses and friends do so effortlessly?

I am in charge of Jacob's care, his schedule and his endless appointments. I am the one who accompanies him to the doctors he hates. I am the one who holds his hand and walks with him in the hallways of the hospitals while we wait for hours for the dreaded visits. And I allow the therapists to subject him to painful and difficult exercises. It's no wonder that he prefers his caregivers, whose main goal is to entertain and please him.

As Jacob's mother, I know he is receiving the care he needs. His frequent screaming in my presence is purely behavioural, designed to manipulate me into giving him what he wants. My heart beats quickly as I run through the list of things that might calm him down, like chasing our cat Spot, helping him strum his red guitar, reading a book or telling him a story.

When nothing else works and I am at a loss for what to try next, I resort to the phone call. At this point, Jacob has been yelling for so long and with such vigor that his face is red and his hair is so wet he looks like he was caught without an umbrella in a rainstorm. Listening to his favourite person, Bracha, on the telephone is a guaranteed mood-changer. It is the one thing that will always calm him down and make him smile.

In my weaker moments, I feel sorry for myself. I am upset that I can't soothe him. I am his mother; I should be his favourite person. But when the crisis is over and peace has been restored, I look at my curly haired child and know that his behaviour is, in some way, typical for a child.

Most parents will agree their children behave better with those who are not their parents. And Jacob, in this respect, is a regular child. Intellectually I know this, but it still hurts. It is heartbreaking to witness someone else pacify my child, something I repeatedly try but fail to do.

Compared to Jacob, his healthy twin sisters are easy to parent. When they are upset or hurt, they run to me. They get angry when I go out and leave them in the care of someone else. As their mommy, I can make everything better. My kisses fix their boo-boos and they love it when I play with them. Why can't I fill the same role for my son?

I try.

One spring day after a stressful doctor visit, I brought Jacob with me to buy a coffee. He enjoyed sitting on my lap, watching the cars drive by the store. Since then, this has become our special outing on our way home from an appointment or when we have a free hour on the weekend.

I look forward to these moments of quiet and peaceful interaction with my son. When I ask if he wants to come for coffee with me, he smiles and slowly nods his head. My heart expands and I feel a whoosh of love for my little boy.

It is hard being the one he associates with the dreaded doctors' appointments. It is challenging to find things Jacob likes to do with me. But I will persist because I love spending happy times with my son. I will keep trying to be the one he wants when he is sad. Because I am his mom.

There are many times when people tell me I'm a great mom but I don't always agree.

I drive my daughters to and from school. I make their meals and give them snacks. I read to them and put them to sleep. When they wake up in the middle of the night, I bring them water, sit on the edge of their beds,and help them get back to sleep.

Jacob gets bussed to school and arrives home while I'm out picking up my girls. Because he can't eat, I have never baked anything for him to taste. A caregiver puts him to bed and a nurse eases him back to sleep if he wakes up before morning.

Over the course of his lifetime, I have amassed an assortment of caregivers, including nurses and nannies. Jake has endeared himself to a growing number of teenagers who love to hang out with him and make him laugh.

And I don't know how they do it. These wonderful saviours spend hours giggling with Jacob and devising creative games with him, week after week. Jake loves their undivided attention and shines in their company.

I watch these people as they lie next to Jacob on the queen-sized mattress in the middle of my living room floor, sharing a joke, and think that they make interacting with my son look so easy and enjoyable.

When I take Jacob out for coffee, we usually have a good time. I prop him on my lap, balancing his head on my shoulder, and we invent stories, look at the cars driving by and people-watch. But when he tires of this activity, my repertoire is depleted and my mind starts racing, running through the short list of things Jacob might like to do with me. Sometimes he will tolerate a short walk but most of the time he starts complaining, his voice quiet at first but then escalating to full-blown screams to let me know he's unhappy. At this point I start to sweat. I hold him or reposition him in his wheelchair, and ask him if he is in pain. During the few minutes it takes for Jake to let me know he is tired of our storytelling until the moment he starts screaming I look at my watch a half dozen times, calculating how long it will be until someone else will be coming to spend time with my son.

When I'm with my daughters I don't watch the clock and wait for someone to relieve me. When they have a day off from school I don't panic if we don't have plans.

Many of my waking hours are devoted to Jacob-related activities. I allot a great deal of time to making sure he receives his medications on time, his nurses are booked, and his endless appointments are scheduled for times that will minimize the disruption to his daily routine.

I am his biggest advocate and I work tirelessly to find ways to improve his communication tools so he can let me know what he wants. His needs are endless and one of my biggest challenges is ensuring they are met. A disproportionate number of my days are Jacob-related yet I don't devote nearly as much time to interacting and playing with my son as I do to his basic needs. And that makes me feel like a bad mom.

Jacob's caregivers have the luxury of dedicating a chunk of time to him. Some have been hired to work with Jacob and are paid to do so. Others have asked for a block of time to be "their" weekly Jacob-time and play with him because of the love they feel for him. Both groups get to go home at the end of their shift and focus on something else.

But I am always thinking about Jacob. About what he requires, what remains to be done, who needs to be contacted. Whether I am with him or not, these thoughts are constantly floating around my mind and they keep me awake at night. But I don't think that's sufficient.

Guilt is a common sentiment expressed by moms. We all seem to believe that we should be doing more and we are all being pulled in so many directions. My daughters have just started Grade One and are in school for the entire day. How will I find enough time to interact with them now? Will they make friends with their classmates? Is this the best school for them? These thoughts are typical of most moms, I think. But my feelings of guilt where Jacob is concerned are different. Intellectually, I know I am doing the best I can and that Jacob is thriving. He is happy, has a lot of friends and is the most loved little boy I know. Emotionally, however, being my son's mother is hard. My heart aches when I watch him struggle to wave his hand or make his thoughts understood. Most things that kids can do so easily, like sitting or holding a toy, are impossible for Jacob. As his mom, I am constantly looking for ways to make Jake's life easier and keep a smile on his chubby face.

And once in a while I do find things he can enjoy. Like our trips to the coffee shop, looking at cat photos and reading Willy Wonka.

I treasure these activities because the special things are so few for him. And our latest discovery was momentous because it signified a victory of sorts.

• • •

To most people it is simply a Cheesie—a tubular, non-nutritious, turn-your-fingers-orange crunchy piece of junk food. But to me it represents so much more.

Food is such an important part of my life. Beyond sustenance, it is a social activity, a time for my family to gather around the kitchen table and catch up on daily activities. It provides a backdrop for getting together with friends and sharing the details of each others' lives, a way to celebrate milestones, and offer support when we are faced with challenges. A birthday party isn't complete until the cake is served. Eating is so much more than simply putting food into our mouths in order to have the energy to live.

Since infancy, Jacob has been fed by a tube inserted directly into his stomach, bypassing his mouth. Eating was lower on my scale of priorities than breathing and Jacob had difficulty with this life-sustaining skill as well. Not being able to nourish my child in the normal way affected me more than I wanted to admit. But I didn't have time to give into my feelings of failure.

Now ten, Jacob is still fed a pre-measured amount of a canned nutritional meal every four hours around the clock. He receives the same thing six times a day, every day. It still takes almost an hour to feed him with a machine that is calibrated to drip 290 drops per hour, slower if he is unwell. Jacob can be fed when he's awake or asleep, lying down or sitting in his wheelchair. For him, it is a passive activity; he doesn't need to do anything.

From the moment his swallowing problem was identified, doctors and feeding therapists encouraged us to let him taste different foods. It started with giving him a pacifier and teaching him to suck.

When Jacob was six months old, the therapist suggested Andrew and I try spoon-feeding him thickened baby cereal. Each day, one of us would place Jacob in his little plastic seat and sit on the floor in front of him. We spooned tiny amounts of clay-coloured mush into his mouth. Unaccustomed to such a sensation, his little tongue would promptly thrust out, expelling the cereal.

We were patient. We tried this several times a day and eventually moved to other flavours. We thought maybe he would like a different variety or brand of cereal so he sampled all the flavours on the supermarket shelf. He seldom lasted more than a few minutes before screaming in protest.

When he was about a year old, Jacob and I were at one of our bi-weekly meetings with the Feeding Therapist at HSC. She asked me if I would object to Jacob tasting a Cheesie. I looked at her and said that I didn't care what he ate—it would simply be amazing for him to be able to enjoy something. Anything. I still held out hope that my son would be able to participate, to some degree, in this basic and social activity. And so, at one year of age, Jacob was introduced to the salty orange snack with no nutritional value. He would tolerate me placing the tip of the Cheesie on his tongue and would even let a bit of the powdery stuff dissolve in his mouth. He didn't hate it, but he certainly didn't like it either.

For the next year or so, I added Cheesies to our limited repertoire of things Jacob could taste. Feeding him this way became one more of his "therapy" goals.

But after several years of painstaking sessions, it became abundantly clear to me that our efforts were futile. He tasted jam, mustard, ketchup, pickles, icing, chocolate and ice cream (what kid doesn't like ice cream?). Jacob didn't like anything and he would often choke on the excess secretions these tasting sessions caused. It wasn't worth risking an aspiration episode for an activity that Jacob didn't even enjoy. I eventually stopped trying to spoon-feed him. I realized that eating did not hold the same meaning for Jacob as it did for me so I moved on to focus on other goals, like finding a way for him to communicate. I didn't dwell on abandoning the feeding goal but anytime a teacher would ask me if Jake could taste something, I experienced a pang of defeat for not being able to teach my son how to eat.

And then, something changed.

One night, nine years after Jacob first tasted rice cereal, our family sat down to dinner. I sliced freshly baked bread and, on a whim, I put a small piece on Jacob's lips. He didn't grimace or move away. Encouraged, I remembered the bags of Cheesies my kids had collected the week before on Halloween and, with some trepidation, brought one out. I placed an orange stick in Jacob's mouth. After a moment of hesitation, Jacob's tongue started moving back and forth—he was licking it! The grimaces I had come to expect were absent. He kept moving his tongue, searching for the food. Andrew and I were laughing and encouraging him. Sierra and Jamie were mesmerized; they had never seen their big brother eat. After sucking all the salty powder off one Cheesie, I asked if he wanted another. He immediately opened his mouth wide, his way of saying yes. He proceeded to eagerly devour two more Cheesies, until his breathing became wheezy and I decided he had enough for one day. I couldn't believe what we were witnessing.

The following day, while his sisters were at a birthday party eating cake and pretzels with their friends, I asked Jacob if he wanted more Cheesies. Again, he said yes. And again, he gobbled them up.

I know Jacob won't ever eat the way the rest of our family does. It isn't safe for him, his vocal cords are still paralyzed and he doesn't crave it. But if he wants to have an after-school snack with his sisters, I will happily feed my son all the Cheesies he can eat (which is usually one or two).

To me, the messy, Styrofoam-textured cylindrical orange puff is not simply a delicious kid-friendly snack. In my heart, it signifies a victory, the achievement of an almost forgotten goal.

But in my mind, it's not enough. It never will be enough.

A family photo: Sierra, Marcy, Jacob, Andrew and Jamie

— JANUARY 2011 —

"Life is what happens to you while you are busy making other plans."

John Lennon

EPILOGUE

I see you sitting on the plastic chair, your big belly straining against the bright pink sweater you wear so often during your pregnancy. As you wait for the nurse to process the paperwork and admit you to the Labor and Delivery department at the hospital so you can be induced, you are anxious and excited about giving birth. As I look back at you, ten years younger than you are today, I wish I could reach out, hold your hand as I peer into your eyes and prepare you for what is coming.

I would tell you that it will be ok, you will be ok. One day, when you don't even realize it, you will see that life has colour again. I can't tell you when it will happen because I don't remember. It wasn't sudden; it was more like a slow realization that you have redefined what happiness and normalcy means. The black and white images that become your life will blend into a beautiful palette of hues. You become stronger, more tolerant and so much wiser. Your priorities will be different and you will be thankful for that.

I know this isn't what you imagined and certainly don't want to hear. You are expecting to leave the hospital tomorrow, with a little bundle wrapped in the same yellow crocheted blanket you were brought home in when you were an infant. You assume you will be awakened during the night by a crying baby needing to eat. You envision toting the little one with you everywhere you want to go, him or her sleeping soundly, oblivious to the hustle of people and the noises around you.

You think you will meet your friends for lunches or walks in the summer, your two-month-old baby content in the little bucket seat that snaps into the folding stroller frame you keep in your car trunk. You expect to be like all your friends who have children, like the families in books or movies. Your life will be picture perfect minus the white picket fence.

If you could to see into your future while waiting for the doctor to induce you, you would know that none of this will happen. Some of the friends you envision cooing over your baby will drop out of your life, unwilling (or unable) to watch what you are dealing with and unsure of how to help. Other people will step up so impressively and you will develop a new appreciation for the meaning of friendship.

But I won't lie; the next few years will be hard. Harder than you think you can handle. They will be devoid of smiles and of happiness. They are going to be filled with worry, the monotonous humming of machines and the ear-piercing screams of pain coming from your little son.

That's right. The people who put their hands on your stomach and confidently stated you are carrying a boy were right. Later today, you will give birth to a six pound eight ounce little boy who isn't so perfect. He will emerge from your body an unnaturally grey color and will have trouble breathing. It will be months before you can take him home and only when you have twenty-four hour nursing care in place. You will not be awakened for middle of the night feedings; instead, you will be roused by ear-piercing cries of pain every time a drop of pumped breast milk drips into the tube that will be surgically implanted into your baby's tummy because his paralyzed vocal cords mean that he can't swallow.

You won't meet your friends for lunch because you will be too busy shuttling Jacob to various appointments. You won't take him for walks in his stroller because he chokes too often. You will coin a new term for yourself called "re-entry" when your mind refocuses on the horror that is your life. You won't go to a movie because the two hours of escape are not worth the agony of re-entry. You won't let yourself forget about the harsh reality at home. You will think it is better to not be distracted than to have to suffer through it again.

It will take years, maybe two, until you become aware that you no longer experience the breath-stealing sensation of re-entry. At some point, you will realize that although Jacob still screams in pain, it won't always be the only sound in your home.

And along the way, when Jacob is almost three years old, you will give birth to twins. A pair of beautiful, healthy girls who share their big brother's gorgeous eyes but not his Pelizaeus-Merzbacher disease, the degenerative disorder that is the root cause of his many health struggles.

When Sierra and Jamie are old enough to move on their own, they will begin to crawl. You will smile when they clamber up to their brother lying on the floor, laugh when they realize he can't move and simply crawl over him. And Jacob will find this so funny that he will laugh along with them.

Jacob will achieve milestones, but they will be ones that are defined for him, not the standard ones used by most people. He will attend school, laugh heartily at funny jokes and attract people like a magnet.

Together, you and Jacob will not let his PMD stop him from doing what other kids do. You will help him bounce a basketball and you will take him to meet the Harlem Globetrotters. You will carry him up a hill so that he can sit on your lap and feel the cold wind whip across his face as he slides to the bottom on a toboggan. And Sierra and Jamie will take turns pushing his wheelchair around the ice as they learn to skate.

And yes, your son will ski. He will sit in a specially-designed contraption and get hoisted onto the chairlift as you watch with a lump of trepidation in your throat. You will stand at the bottom of the hill in below-zero cold with your video camera, ready to catch a shot of him zooming by on the way back to the chairlift for another run. And the enormous grin and big white teeth will be the only things you can see on his goggle-covered face. By the end of the season, you will be the one positioned behind his sit-ski, skiing him down the hill, listening to his screams of exuberance as you gain speed and hurtle over a bump.

He will learn to swim and be great at it. With the aid of a purple Lifesaver candy shaped ring around his neck to keep his head out of the water, Jacob will kick his legs and doggie paddle 200 meters in the pool each week. All eyes will be on him when he squeals with excitement. You will receive an email from Danielle, a film student and part-time lifeguard that reads: *Last year I worked on Thursday nights, guarding during the half hour that Jacob swam with Larissa, and every single night I would become completely hypnotized with the two of them in the water. I even had the pleasure of swimming with Jacob on one of the nights that Larissa was not feeling well, and it was one of the greatest experiences I have ever had.* Danielle and her classmates will make a documentary about your son and his swimming ability because of how he mesmerized her each time she watched him in the water.

Jacob will be a source of inspiration to so many and a bright light in your life. I know it is hard to see now, but trust me, he will be happy. Your son will teach you how to be a parent and you will protect and advocate for him every chance you get. You will walk down the street, pushing his wheelchair, talking to your son, and trying to ignore the sympathetic glances of strangers. You will stand tall and show everyone that you are proud to be his mother.

Your first born child will have an awesome sense of humour and very definitive likes and dislikes. You will smile every time you see the sparkle in his eyes when he watches his favourite cat jump on his bed at night. You will marvel at his persistence, his strength and his determination.

You will kneel next to Jacob in his wheelchair on his tenth birthday as he listens to a room full of people sing Happy Birthday. And you will be in awe of how much your son has accomplished and wonder how many more feats he will achieve in his second decade.

Marcy and Jacob at Jacob's 10th birthday party

— MAY 15, 2012 —

ACKNOWLEDGEMENTS

This book took many years to complete. At times, it was brutally hard to relive our early struggles and detail the challenges we faced. But the happy times reminded me of all the amazing people who helped shape our story:

Bracha, whose dedication to Jacob hasn't wavered despite the geographical distance that now separates them.

Jacob's many princesses whose numbers continue to grow but still include Sar-G, Rivky, Batsheva, Shoshana, Tzipporah, Ricky, Leah and Yaffi.

Devorah Vale, Jacob's first teacher to recognize and nurture my son's ability to learn.

Cheryl Libman, unequivocally the most incredible, loving and dedicated educator and friend.

Dr. James Garbern, whose irreplaceable knowledge and commitment to all of his PMD families is sorely missed.

Tom Chau who is responsible for giving Jacob a voice.

Jeff and Ellen Schwartz for sharing their experiences and letting us work with Jacob's Ladder.

Louise Kinross for letting me learn from her and Ben.

Laura Rosen-Cohen for always understanding and commiserating with me.

Robin Stone, Christine Biggs and Elizabeth Brooks for reading, critiquing and refining this book over countless coffees and salads.

Arnold Gosewich for blunt feedback and for introducing me to Linda Pruessen and her insightful editing.

Shelley Thierrault for copyediting and encouragement.

And finally, Andrew, Sierra and Jamie. This story wouldn't be the same without you.

ABOUT THE AUTHOR

MARCY WHITE BSc, MSW, MBA, enjoyed a career in the investment industry until her son, Jacob was born in 2002. Her academic degrees did not prepare her for caring for Jacob, who was born with Pelizaeus-Merzbacher disease (PMD). Since Jacob's diagnosis at ten months old, Marcy has become an advocate for her son and furthering PMD research to help find a cure. Marcy has published many articles about Jacob that have appeared in such publications as *The Globe and Mail*, *Canadian Jewish News* and *Exceptional Parent*. She co-founded **www.curepmd.com** to educate people about PMD and fund research into finding a treatment. Marcy lives in Toronto with her husband, Andrew, and their three children, Jacob, Sierra and Jamie.

CPSIA information can be obtained at www.ICGtesting.com
Printed in the USA
LVOW11s0031030214

371855LV00004B/12/P

9 780992 143602